A NIGHT
AT THE OPERA

'The greatest singers in the world do not fit easily into blue jeans' (Sir Rudolph Bing)

A NIGHT
AT THE OPERA

Edited and compiled by Barry Hewlett-Davies

Foreword by the Earl of Harewood

Illustrations by Lucy

WEIDENFELD AND NICOLSON
LONDON

For Rita and Alberto

This collection copyright © Barry Hewlett-Davies 1980
All royalties to the English National Opera and Sadler's Wells Benevolent
Fund.

ISBN 0 297 77820 X

Set, printed and bound in Great Britain by
Fakenham Press Limited, Fakenham, Norfolk

Contents

Preface

BARRY HEWLETT-DAVIES

'Funny moments in opera?'

'Yes.'

'Funny?'

'Yes. You know. In opera.'

'Ah! Tell you what – you ought to go round and see old – er – Roland. Used to be in the chorus. He'll tell you a thing or two. Has us all in stitches once he gets going. Get him to tell you about the night the portcullis fell on the tenor in – what was it? No. Not *The Barber of Seville*, don't recall a portcullis in *The Barber* – no; you go and see old – er. Loads of funny stories. Terribly funny bloke ... probably find him round the Lemon Tree about this time.'

When you eventually meet er-Roland, he might well (a) be saving himself for his own book (legitimate reticence – kindly keep off), (b) be suffering from an attack of amnesia (usual opening gambit: 'I'm drinking large brandies with soda, if that's all right, old son'), or (c) suddenly be transformed into a sort of Vincent Price of the world of opera, which performance will cause all the other people in the pub to fall about in hysterics but will reduce you to a scarlet-faced wreck as he stands, apparently eight feet high, on the table to demonstrate how they backed the ship in *The Flying Dutchman*.

As it was, nothing like that happened to me while I was compiling this book.

Almost everyone I approached was helpful. There were one or two embarrassing failures based on false information. I am not prepared to talk about them but I have apologized to the people concerned.

It has taken two years for this book to come together. Unexpectedly funny moments are not all that easy to come by, nor indeed are they particularly frequent in these days of increased acting skills on the part of opera singers and less obtrusive technical innovations in the theatre.

There is also the problem of transcription: someone who can turn a room full of people into helpless gigglers does not always come alive on the page.

The idea for the book came to a friend and myself after we had seen, well, I suppose you might call him a slightly sub-standard stand-in at the last moment for the tenor lead. He looked happy enough (indeed, he never stopped smiling) but it was instantly obvious that he did not know his way around the stage, there having been no time to rehearse him. There was no ill will in the audience towards him, quite the opposite, but none the less an inevitable tension built up and we waited, fascinated, *willing* him not to do anything unforgivable. And he didn't.

He neither fell over the furniture nor caused anyone else to: his trousers stayed up; he didn't exit through a fireplace, and he didn't stand on the soprano's frock. But it was the awareness that this little figure might have brought about practically any disaster that kept us covering his every move. His only real 'sin' was that for quite lengthy periods he was unlit because he couldn't find the light (as we say in the business) and, to be honest, he was not the man we were expecting, vocally.

The company was marvellously protective towards him and anyone unkind enough to have it in mind to boo his curtain calls was thwarted because he always appeared between two stars, each holding a hand.

From that evening came the idea for this book. I hope that nothing in it will give offence. An art form as superb as opera should not be tittered at lightly.

Foreword

THE EARL OF HAREWOOD
MANAGING DIRECTOR,
ENGLISH NATIONAL OPERA

I hope that everyone who reads this book will be entertained and amused by it and perhaps those who aren't yet opera-goers will be encouraged to begin.

Actually, quite a lot of opera goes on without these disasters, difficult as it is to put on three or four different performances every week, each as complicated as a big West End show and each judged as critically. But, as with true tragedy, operatic figures aspire to such heights of nobility that the falls are cataclismically great and therefore correspondingly funny. I hope you agree.

Harewood

(Back-stage notice)

> NO SMILING ON-STAGE, PLEASE
> PURGATORY THIS WAY →

Hardy Amies

COUTURIER

In the dim sad days long ago when opera was being coaxed into flower at Covent Garden, there was a production of *Der Freischütz*.

My recollection is that opera sung in its original tongue had already begun to infiltrate into the repertoire so we were all a little surprised to find that we had gone back to singing in English. Possibly this was because the girl who sang Anna, was, I think, American.

The libretto of *Der Freischütz* is not easily acceptable in any circumstances. The scenery and production were far from new; the *naïveté* of the libretto caused ripples of unease throughout the whole evening only subdued by the politeness usual to the Covent Garden audience.

However by Act III we were no longer able to contain ourselves and loud laughter greeted the opening words of Anna (or rather Annchen's) *Romanze und Aria* which were:

> *One night my Auntie lay a-dreaming*
> *When all at once the door swung wide*
> *And something big and white and gleaming*
> *Came creeping over to her side.*

The evening drew to a close amid ironic cheers.

John Julius,
Viscount Norwich

WRITER AND BROADCASTER

By far the most enjoyable of the unintentionally funny moments that I remember occurred in Turin during a performance of *Rigoletto*. The gallery was, as far as I remember, full of football supporters who had been at some match that afternoon, and during the second interval one of them inadvertently (I think) let go

of the string of a large gas balloon that he had been holding under his seat.

It went straight up to the ceiling, which was a mildly amusing thing to happen but not particularly worrying; but then, half-way through the last act, we were suddenly aware that it had left the ceiling and was slowly losing height.

At the same time some gentle draught was blowing it, equally slowly but inexorably forward towards the stage. The thunderstorm was beginning and the action rapidly approaching its tragic climax; but by now the eyes of every member of the audience and cast were fixed on this terrible approaching balloon. It was, as I remember, bright yellow. There seemed no way of reaching it until it actually crossed the footlights, by which time the dramatic tension – or what remained of it – would have been utterly destroyed.

Then, at the last moment, it drifted lower over the orchestra pit, and the bassoonist managed to reach up with his instrument and hooked it down with the mouthpiece.

As he hauled it down to safety there rose from the audience the mightiest cheer that I have ever heard – but they were, of course, a football crowd.

And the show went on.

Sir Harold Wilson

FORMER PRIME MINISTER

One of W. S. Gilbert's jokes was to include among the principals of
HMS Pinafore the Midshipmite – the smallest of the midshipmen
who neither says nor sings a word. By being cast as the Midshipmite I therefore, at the age of ten, had a principal's role in Gilbert
and Sullivan. And a most embarrassing experience it turned out to
be.

The production by the Milnsbridge Baptist Amateur Operatic
Society had six performances. My father, as secretary of the
society, was determined to get full value from what he regarded as
the outrageous payment of two guineas royalty to the Savoy
Operas.

At each of the performances the girl playing Little Buttercup
arrived with a different basket of goodies for the Midshipmite. On
the first night, even I realized that the large triangular-section bar
of Toblerone was a bit of an anachronism.

On the second night Little Buttercup arrived with an entirely
modern shopping bag containing thoroughly traditional humbugs
– very large ones. It was only a little later, as I stood to attention
during one of the saddest moments of the opera, that I suddenly
realized that the eyes of the entire cast and, indeed, the audience,
seemed to be on me.

It was either my noisy sucking of the humbug or the fact that it
made my left cheek stick out a good three inches more than the
other.

The action froze as Miss Hylands, the producer, stormed into the
wings, seized me by the hand and dragged me off the stage. And I
am convinced everyone heard her shout: *'Spit it out at once!'*

Aida on tour

Sir John Barbirolli once conducted *Aida* in Leeds in one of those theatres which are absolutely charming front of house, all red plush and gilt and painted panels, but absolute hell backstage for the folk working there. A novel feature of this house was that the plumbing (untouched by any plumber's hand since its installation in the late eighties) dictated that the women in the chorus had to accommodate themselves in a little cabinet directly above the prompt side.

The opera went more or less its usual course till the last act when Radames sang his unaccompanied recitative 'Aida, where art thou . . . ?' – at which someone flushed the ancient loo with appropriate Verdian vigour.

'I'm afraid the opera ended there,' Barbirolli recalled afterwards, 'though we did continue gallantly to the end.'

At a Covent Garden touring production of *Aida* in Oxford Radames and Aida were in their vault, the tomb doors were closing slowly, ladies in the stalls were dabbing their eyes with their handkerchiefs and undergraduates in the gods were preparing to go home, everything was happening as it should, in other words – except there was something funny about the tomb doors. Instead of stopping when they met, they continued on their separate tracks so they passed one another like silent stately tramcars until the left-hand door went off stage-right and vice versa. An over-enthusiastic part-time stage hand was seeing how far the doors would go. He found out. In the meantime, hero and heroine stood immobile in their final clinch for what seemed like an hour until it occurred to the man on the switchboard to bring in a slow black-out.

Rita Hunter

ENGLISH NATIONAL OPERA AND INTERNATIONAL SOPRANO

I was in New Orleans to sing my first Abigaille in *Nabucco* and the producer, a great guy called Jim Lucas, had decided to have Nabucco make his first big entrance on the back of a great big horse.

She was a beautiful black mare called Sunny. Everything was going okay until the dress rehearsal, with, I must add, an invited audience, full orchestral sound and chorus. Alas, the excitement was too much for darling Sunny who promptly did a million 'whoopsies' all over the stage.

I went to step to the front to join in the big ensemble, doing my

Lucy.

best to ignore Sunny's indiscretions, when the producer suddenly screamed: 'Hunter! For god's sake, don't move! Don't move an inch! Think of your train!'

So I stood still – and got the giggles which, of course, set everyone else off.

Poor Jim Lucas was still shouting, 'Get a shovel someone, get a shovel, can't you?'

A little black man popped up from somewhere and shouted back: 'Honey chil', we ain't got no shovel!'

The orchestra had by now gone to pieces and most of the house seemed to be in hysterics. But above the uproar you could still hear Jim bellowing: 'God help me, don't you know you never hire a horse without a shovel?!'

Glen Byam Shaw

CONSULTANT DIRECTOR, ENGLISH NATIONAL OPERA

Nigel Playfair was sitting in his office at the Lyric Theatre, Hammersmith, one afternoon before a new production of his was about to open when, without warning, the door flew open and one of the leading ladies stalked in.

'This is an outrage, Nigel!' she said. 'Quite outrageous!'

Playfair asked what the matter was.

'The billing, Nigel, the billing. MY name should be at the top, not underneath that other person's.'

'Ah', said Playfair. 'I'm afraid I cannot help you. I don't do the billing. I do the coo-ing.'

The lady left the office less dramatically than she came in.

Roger Prout

FORMERLY WELSH NATIONAL OPERA COMPANY

In 1967 we had just opened a new production of Don Pasquale at the New Theatre in Cardiff. A party had been laid on for the senior members of the company at a local hotel but admission was limited to the principal singers, trustees, and administration mandarins. The rest of us, including a then very new conductor, Nicholas Braithwaite, were left floating on a post-performance high, with nowhere to go. I had a flat in Cardiff at that time and invited the *hoi polloi* back on a bring-your-own-bottle basis.

My flat-mate in those days was John Sanders, an ex-medical student (now a magazine editor) who had just returned from a stage design course in Vienna and had taken a temporary job as a bus conductor.

John came home from late shift, found the flat overflowing with people, so rushed into his room to change. Mingling with the party in his best suit, John wandered somewhere in the vicinity of Nicky Braithwaite. Someone asked him what he did for a living. John simply said he was a conductor – and a number of eyes promptly focused on him. Nick walked over to him. A most remarkable conversation followed. They treated each other somewhat cautiously, each obviously feeling that the other's name should be familiar but unable to place the face.

'I'm a conductor, too,' said Nicky. 'What are you doing at the moment?'

'I'm on the Pavilion run,' said John. (The pavilion at Sophia Gardens, Cardiff, as well as being a bus-stop is also a huge hall used for concerts.)

Nick looked terribly impressed and the conversation rolled on with small talk. A good two or three minutes elapsed before John

baffled Nick with a question about which run *he* was on.

I had a slightly bizarre moment in connection with our production of *Tosca*. In an idle moment I sat down to clean up the hired muskets newly arrived from the suppliers. My stage director came flying past and told me not to bother because there were more important things to do. I lingered long enough to finish the one I had started and found that there was a broken ramrod lodged in the barrel. Had it gone unnoticed the gun would have been used with a blank cartridge two hours later by the firing squad who execute Cavaradossi with more than the usual degree of realism.

Talking about realism: Elizabeth Vaughan has the best cough in the business. During her first season with us in *La Bohème* I passed her in the dressing-room corridor apparently coughing her last. I dived into the nearest dressing-room and rushed back to her with a glass of water. 'It's all right,' she said with a smile. 'I was just practising.'

Liz Vaughan, along with Anne Howells and so many modern sopranos are a far cry from the popular image of the diva. Janet Hughes, the Glyndebourne mezzo, mentioned an odd incident with her piano. She wanted it moved from Liverpool to London and engaged a removal firm who sent along two burly Liverpudlians to carry out the job.

One of them asked Janet if she was a singer and she explained that she sang in opera.

They would have none of that: 'Yer can't be an opera singer, luv – you ain't fat enough nor ugly!'

I read somewhere that Signora Puccini took unkindly to her husband mixing with good-looking young sops and mezzos and so apparently used to safeguard her interests by putting extra garlic into Puccini's food before he left for the theatre. This reminds me that I took Milla Andrew for her first curry lunch just before a matinée performance of *Il Tabarro*. Throughout *'Ma chi lascia il sobborgo'* Luigi (John Andrew) wore a glazed smile until he was able to move to leeward.

Returning to the Welsh National's *Don Pasquale*: while that show was in rehearsal we were staging a revival of *Don Giovanni*. Giovanni was sung by Forbes Robinson, Leporello by John Gibbs. Evidently the producer, Michael Geliot, had chosen to use his biggest guns on the title role rather than the popular preference for giving Leporello's part to the star guest. In any event, John Gibbs developed throat trouble.

With only hours to go before curtain up, our administrator decided to approach Sir Geraint Evans who was, at that time, on his way down to us from London for the Pasquale call. Geraint was on his first season with his own 'national' company and being very co-operative, as indeed he always is. (His Welsh accent used to jump from the near negligible to overpowering whenever he passed the stage door in Cardiff!)

Geraint, internationally well known and acclaimed for Leporello, squeezed into John Gibb's costume and went on. The production was in English. Geraint knew it only in Italian.

Our designs (by Annena Stubbs) involved flying in odd bits of scenery in a highly original presentation. Ordinarily singers are used to being pitched into productions at short notice from time to time, but this was not one which lent itself readily to newcomers. The result was a devastatingly funny performance. Singers of lesser ability than Geraint Evans and Forbes Robinson might have been content with a workmanlike performance to bridge a difficult evening. But both went far beyond that. They excelled themselves.

Geraint Evans would enter and a new piece of scenery would drop promptly and take him out of sight . . . the Don and Leporello frequently lost each other completely in the maze of scenic bits and pieces, popping up in front of each other without warning. Geraint would manage to translate the odd passage or two ad lib into English only to find that Forbes had now switched to Italian. The lyrics have never been more happily abused. Snippets of Welsh, shouted directions: 'Watch out for your head!' were joined by curious new lines like: 'Best of luck to you an' all, Butty' and there were various references to the Triple Crown (Wales had lost a major rugby match and most of the nation was in mourning).

I was 'in the corner' that evening, getting terribly harassed by a performance which threatened to get out of hand any moment. Inevitably, I missed giving the lighting man one of his cues. The cue was one which would have brought on a light in a window. The window was the object of Giovanni's attention during the canzonetta 'Deh vieni'. Forbes had simply stopped singing and was staring up at the darkened window clicking his fingers at it. I hastily hit the light cue, just as Forbes kicked the set. The light came on as if in response to his boot and the audience dissolved into laughter.

Touring *Die Fledermaus* is always a dreadful problem for the stage management. The show always involves much glassware and hired hands are never gentle with skips. Each new venue meant finding replacement bits and pieces. After trailing round Swansea on a wet Bank Holiday looking for sixteen champagne glasses and a flambeau glass lampshade to replace breakages, I felt that drastic countermeasures were in order.

I had already tried putting all the glass in one skip marked 'FRAGILE. DO NOT DROP' and that sort of thing, but it seemed to act as an incentive for even more hefty handling.

Then I had an idea.

I painted the skip which held the glass bright red, painted out all references to glass, looked up the chemical formula for glass and made out a new notice:

$$Na_2\ SiO_3/Ca\ Si\ O_3$$

HANDLE WITH EXTREME CARE
DO NOT SMOKE

It did the trick. I lost no more glassware in transit after that.

Properties frequently cause peculiar incidents. In our production of *La Bohème* I was asked to provide a fish that could be thrown around the stage by the bohemians before they ate it. I boiled the fish on a gas ring in the stage door-keeper's office but was waylaid by some passing crisis and briefly forgot about it. That evening Clifford Grant hurled it across the set and Michael Maurel disappeared in a blizzard of atomized trout. We went back to a fish stuffed with canvas after that.

Just before that new production of *Bohème* (it was by John Copley) I visited Musetta in her dressing-room to explain the operation of a new trick – a prop involving a bunch of flowers. Musetta listened, or at least seemed to, while she changed. Eventually she stood contemplating the bunch of flowers – with no clothes on at all.

She stared at me, dived across the room and flung the flowers in a heap.

'I thought you were my husband!' she yelled. 'Get out!'

I never quite worked that out. Pre-performance tension causes some extraordinary things to happen.

Tab cues can cause total disruption of an opera. Soon after I left the Welsh National my replacement brought down the curtain too soon on Act II of *Tosca*. Tosca (Milla Andrew) had just said of the dead Scarpia: 'This is the man at whose feet all Rome trembled' – and down it came.

It was promptly taken back up again to reveal a bewildered Tosca helping Scarpia back on to his feet. He was facing the curtain and with great presence of mind, let out an agonized moan and fell back to the ground. Tosca whirled round and started her line again just as the obviously panic-striken tabs operator brought down the curtain again. The orchestra had just started to play and fell apart. The curtain stayed down after that.

A passing thought on which to close: while stage-managing in opera, my party trick was to tell back-stage visitors that on a given cue they would see handkerchiefs come out all over the theatre. I'd send the visitor to a peep-hole at the climax of *Butterfly*, *Traviata* and *Bohème* and the audience always obliged.

Come to think of it, during one season I always kept a small area clear near my corner for our van drivers, two strapping great Welshmen, who loved to watch the last acts of those operas at every performance, tears running down their cheeks.

'Lovely, bloody lovely,' was all they ever said.

A performance of *The Bartered Bride* at Swansea Grand involved us in hiring a bearskin costume. A wonderfully realistic piece of work it was, too. We persuaded an ASM to put it on and come over the road for a pint. We *had* expected the sight of a bear downing a pint of best bitter to cause a little excitement in the British Volunteer.

Nobody gave him a second glance.

We should have known. Regulars at a stage door pub are so used to the sight of tippling men in armour and the like that no visitor to the pub can hope to generate any interest at all.

The Bartered Bride was a show in which I nearly had my cards. The tabs cue at the end of Act I was four bars late. The ballet were whirling like dervishes and could keep it up for only another two bars from the cue. The new electrically operated curtain (the cause of the trouble) dropped majestically on a floundering heap of arms and legs.

During the same production, Anne Pashley at the dress rehearsal had her first one-hand lift by the leading male dancer. Clutching her 'Esmeralda' parasol she rose gracefully a good eight feet above the stage before squealing: 'No! Not *there*!', straightening out to a horizontal position and falling off.

Lucien Muratore
bedevilled

In the South of France some years ago I was singing Faust with a Mephisto who had a splendid voice but rather unusual measurements – you could say without malice that he was as broad as he was long. In Act I he had to come up through a trap to the accompaniment of smoke and magnesium flares.

I had just finished the opening invocation, *'À moi, Satan, à moi'*, when the trap opened and Satan's top half appeared but the rest of him emerged with such difficulty that the lower half of his costume was disastrously and revealingly torn.

Mephisto, suspecting nothing, continued in a voice of thunder, *'D'où vient ta surprise? Ne suis-je pas mis à ta guise?'* ['Why do you start as you greet me? Does it frighten you to see me?']

The curtain had to be lowered for the sake of decency. One woman was reported fainted – the rest of the house rocked with laughter.

From *Petites Histoires de la Grande Musique* by Pierre Hegel (Editions La Clé d'Or, 1977); this extract translated by Lionel Lethbridge.

Opera Buffa

Danny O'Mara, an Irish baritone, was playing Covent Garden in *Fidelio* – or at any rate, in some piece which required his being in prison. Mrs O'Mara and their children were staying at an hotel a short distance away and she used to take them to say goodnight to their father in his dressing-room between acts.

Going back to their hotel in a crowded bus one evening, one of the children demanded to know in his loudest possible voice: 'Why is it, every time we go to see Daddy, he's always in prison?'

For the rest of the journey scarlet Mrs O'Mara was left in no doubt what the English felt about Irish immigrants.

At a performance of a piece called, *The Lily of Killarny* in Tullamore, Danny was the villain and had to throw the heroine Eily O'Connor into the sea. This effect was meant to be achieved by his thrusting her heftily into the wings where a stage-hand was waiting to drop a large stone into a tub of water to make the necessary splash.

The stage-hand wasn't looking at what he was doing and missed his aim. The stone hit the floor with a thud and bounced on to his foot.

Danny O'Mara, a man of infinite resource, turned to the audience with an expression of extreme disgust and said: 'Would you believe that, now – frozen, by God!'

Since the plot demands that he is immediately shot and falls into the sea himself, he had no alternative but to throw himself into the wings – in silence.

John Copley

PRODUCER, ROYAL OPERA HOUSE AND ENGLISH NATIONAL OPERA

When I was very happily assisting Franco Zeffirelli in the Covent Garden production of *Don Giovanni*, I had, quite unexpectedly, to stand in in Act II for Cesare Siepi who had unfortunately been hit over the head by a piece of scenery in the finale to Act I.

The first recitative with Sir Geraint Evans went well but then Sir George Solti insisted that I sang the serenade as he needed to adjust the amplification of the off-stage mandolin.

Now, I've never felt Don Giovanni to be one of my greatest roles! But I did what had to be done. Quite unknown to me, the late Sir David Webster had brought Otto Klemperer to watch the rehearsal.

After a few lines of my devastating singing of *'Deh, vieni alla finistra'*, Dr Klemperer turned to Sir David and said: 'This Don Giovanni is terrible!'

It was then explained to him that I was the assistant to the producer. There was a long pause. And then Klemperer said:

'But he's still *terrrrible!*'

International affairs
and Sir Malcolm Sargent

Sir Malcolm, while on a concert tour in Israel, asked to see the disputed territory of the Gaza Strip. A visit was duly arranged, during the course of which the jeep in which he was travelling was shelled from the Arab side and Sir Malcolm escaped injury only narrowly.

Back home, on being told what had happened, Sir Thomas Beecham commented, 'I had no idea the Arabs took music so seriously.'

It was also Sargent who after one first night made his way to the royal box and said proudly: 'Your Majesty, may I introduce Sergio Poliakoff . . . Sergio . . . this is the King of Norway!'

The royal figure bowed slightly and murmured, 'Sweden, actually.'

Roy Dawson Gubby

COMPOSER

I was manning a Bofors gun in the middle of Salisbury Plain at the beginning of the Second World War, but none the less found myself roped into the Southern Command Symphony Orchestra which Eric Fenby had been detailed to conduct, somewhat against his will. It was an odd experience to turn up for a first rehearsal in a strange army building full of unidentified musicians – many of them Jews who were still German and who were to remain so until the end of the war. (They were officially in the Royal Pioneer Corps but always referred to themselves as 'The King's Own Enemies'.)

However, once the rehearsal was under way, I found myself back in the pre-war world of music with its courteous refinements and general air of 'culture' – all very different from life on the gun site. All was going well with our playing the ballet music from *Eugene Onegin* but ... I don't know ... something wasn't quite right. Ah! That was it. No trumpeters. They hadn't turned up.

When they did, we all wished they hadn't bothered. They were under orders to attend and had probably never set eyes on a symphonic score in their lives. Their intonation was, well, vile.

Eric Fenby stopped the music with a sigh and a diffident cough. Hesitantly he suggested that perhaps *that* young man over there could pitch his note just a *little* higher ... ?

The young man in question was standing no nonsense and stood up to say as much. 'It's all bloody well for you, mister,' he said, 'but it's bloody cold in this bleedin' shed!'

In the brief silence which followed, the pre-war courtesy vanished and Salisbury Plain seemed more like Burnham Wood than ever. Gloom descended on Fenby, myself and the King's Own Enemies alike. So much for escapism.

We were rescued by the man in charge of the trumpeters. He leaped to his feet and rounded on his chilly colleague.

'Sonny,' he said. 'Just you get on and blow that — thing. And *bloody well play it in tune*!'

Fenby paused for a moment. He picked up his baton. He allowed himself a little smile. 'Gentlemen,' he said 'Shall we start again at the letter A?'

The world of music had returned, if only temporarily.

At one time, soldiers on evenings off used to walk on as extras for a pound a time. One particular evening, two Scots Guardsmen rolled up – literally, having come by way of all the pubs from their barracks.

They gathered the opera was *Samson and Delilah* (it might as well have been Tom and Jerry for all they knew) and having drawn their costumes and received their few directions from the producer, they waited for someone to shove them on-stage at the right moment.

The right moment, as far as they were concerned, was the temple scene where, dressed as Philistine soldiers, they stood to attention,

each holding a spear, one each side of the foot of the great staircase. One soldier was slightly more sober than his friend, and gave him one or two anxious glances. Something was not quite right. The friend was standing bolt upright, rigidly to attention, but was apparently incapable of response.

The truth dawned – the other soldier was out on his feet. All too soon came the climax. Samson put his shoulders to the pillars of the temple and shoved. The collapse was not shown. The lights were cut instead and a cloth lowered showing the temple in ruins; everyone on-stage lay down dead.

The lights came up. The more sober guardsman looked round for his mate and surreptitiously raised his head. There stood his friend, still at attention – 'the sole bloody survivor!'

After the war I remember attending a full rehearsal of *Aida* with Sir Thomas Beecham. It did not go well. The organ was too loud, not once but twice. A dignified contretemps ensued. Sir Thomas turned to the organist. The organist referred the matter to an engineer.

'Ask him to come up,' suggested Sir Thomas.

An apprehensive man duly appeared. The difficulty was explained to him. In turn he ordered a technician to 'regulate it to number four'.

The rehearsal began again. Sir Thomas then felt that the lead tenor, a singer of international repute, not easily persuaded, was not giving of his best. He listened to Sir Thomas's advice but did nothing to improve the less than cordial atmosphere by standing in front of the conductor, eyebrows raised in apparently amazed incredulity.

The final show-down came with a group of on-stage trumpeters from the Royal Military School of Music who seemed to be going their own way as far as tempo was concerned. The rehearsal stopped once more and Sir Thomas asked for an explanation.

It was the fault of the scenery, according to the stage manager. It had been set in such a way that the trumpeters could not see Beecham's baton.

'Then *move* the set!' cried Beecham. 'It's your job, not mine. I'm only in charge of the *pit*!'

Puccini master-class

Giacomo Puccini, at an hotel in Milan, was infuriated to hear *'Un bel di'* played by a barrel-organ in the street beneath his window. What upset him was not that his music was being played by an inappropriate instrument, but that the operator was playing it too slowly.

Puccini came to a decision. The people of Milan deserved something better, and, he, the composer, was going to see that they got it.

He flung open the doors of his apartment, rushed down the stairs, pushing out of his way servants and guests alike. On reaching the street he pushed his way to the organ-grinder, grabbed the handle of the machine and began to turn it like mad.

'There!' he snapped. *'That* is the proper tempo. Don't you ever let me hear you playing it any other way again.'

The next day, the organ-grinder was on his pitch outside the hotel once more. But this time there was a notice displayed on his instrument. It said:

> PUPIL OF PUCCINI

Monica Lera

FORMER MEMBER OF THE OPERA HOUSE BALLET

My first experience of the opera ballet, and the highlight of the repertoire, was the first performance of *Koanga* by Delius which was well-received by London audiences and critics but much less so in Bradford – which, of course, is where Delius was born. Sir Thomas Beecham, who was conducting, told the *Yorkshire Post*: 'Why should I come to Bradford? I go to Berlin and you cannot get in. I go to America and you cannot get in. Here in Bradford we play a splendid work of my greatest friend and you do not *come* in. I consider it to be an insult to the memory of a great man. I question whether I shall ever return to this town to conduct opera.'

During this tour, *Un Ballo in Maschera*, *Il Barbiere* and *La Bohème* were sung in Italian and *Der Freischütz* and *Siegfried* in German. The ASM and some members of the chorus had been in the Carl Rosa for many years and some of the older members, though going through the motions of singing in Italian or German at rehearsals, reverted to English in performance, which sounded distinctly odd. The ASM took every opportunity he could of singing the arias in the wings in English at the same time that Heddle Nash was singing Rodolfo in Italian or Walter Widdop was singing Siegfried in German. There was a strong Carl Rosa lobby of contempt for singing in those foreign lingos!

In those pre-television days, when an off-stage chorus was needed in an opera, its conductor used to look through a hole in the backcloth to synchronize his beat with the conductor in the pit. There were many holes in the ancient backcloths at Covent Garden in those days, but one season a new cloth was painted for a new production of *The Ring* cycle.

At the first full rehearsal on stage, the off-stage chorus assembled and their conductor mounted a step ladder and searched for a hole in the new cloth.

Furious at not finding one, and quite unaware of the enormity of his offence, he took out a penknife and cut himself a satisfactory hole. The rehearsal got under way. The stage director, Charles Moor, left the prompt corner to see that all was well. I was waiting in the wings with the other dancers when Charles Moor caught sight of the off-stage conductor on the top of his step-ladder, right eye firmly fixed through the illicit hole, giving the beat to the singers behind him.

With waves of Wagner surging all around on and off stage, Charles, red-faced with rage at the desecration of his precious backcloth, ordered it to be lowered immediately for repairs. The fly-men obeyed instantly, the cloth was lowered for repair, leaving the off-stage conductor looking extremely foolish on top of his ladder.

The International season included *Die Meistersinger*, in which the young Swedish tenor Torsten Ralk made his début as Walther. A critic wrote: 'It was a relief to have a knight of such confident valour for whom the competitive festival (save for one unlucky slip before the end) held no terrors.'

That unlucky slip looked very different when seen at close quarters. I was sitting on a rostrum up-stage. When Torsten came to sing the Prize Song, all went well at first, but, then – quite suddenly – he forgot the words. The back of his neck went quite red while he lah-lahed his way through the melody with Sir Thomas casting him evil looks from the pit. The poor prompter nearly went crazy, shouting, not whispering the words to him and became so het up I thought he was going to leap out of the prompt box and sing the part himself! All this probably happened within a very few bars of music but to us, on-stage, it seemed like eternity until poor Walther recollected his lines.

On tour with *La Bohème* we dancers were used as children and street urchins in Act II outside the Café Momus. The very nice real food provided for Musetta and her friends was very attractive to dancers on tour trying to live on a low wage. We used to wait in the wings, waiting for the food to be cleared off the tables and then fall upon it, stuffing slices of ham, cream cakes and rolls down the front of our costumes. We then had to make our entrance, skipping and dancing about like small children with our precious spoils melting and oozing through our skirts and pinafores. The stage manager's eye had to be avoided at all costs.

Still on food, in *Parsifal* we were acolytes for the Grail scene. We had to deliver small buns to the Knights of the Grail, handing one to each Knight very solemnly. Waiting in the wings, holding our trays of buns, we whiled away the time by nibbling a small bite out of each one. We made our entrance in procession and as the *Parsifal* leitmotiv rang out, we slowly circled the long table, handing out the buns with reverent gestures while the Knights muttered: 'The rats have been at this. I shall complain to the management!' all *sotto voce* with expressions of deep devotion on their faces.

Sir Thomas both produced and conducted *The Tales of Hoffman*. After the dress rehearsal he decided that the Spalanzani scene needed more movement and decided to have a small boy ride across the stage on a velocipede. I was chosen for this important role and a rehearsal with Sir Thomas was arranged. I waited trembling in the wings, a stage-hand holding the velocipede at the ready (which looked extremely dangerous), and then suddenly the great man appeared, a small dapper figure in an opera hat and black cloak.

'My deah young lady, you take the machine – so.' He took it from the stage-hand, nimbly threw his leg across it: 'And off you go.' He shot across the stage with the stage-hand in pursuit, reached the other side, dismounted, and disappeared without saying another word.

I managed to get the hang of it and did not fall off on the first night but I had the uncomfortable feeling that my intrepid ride was not noticed by anybody. I think I received an extra two shillings; dancers always got a bit extra if they had to do something which wasn't dancing.

The most coveted role was the body in the bag in *Rigoletto*, for which you got three shillings and sixpence but the ASM's wife always got that.

An opera boy

'I'm an opera boy, you know. Not a tremendous Wagnerian on account of getting fidgety, but I love Verdi and Donizetti and all those buxom prima donnas [*sic*] and all the carry-ons and the rows and refusing to take curtain calls. I love it!'

I think we must face the fact
That Carmen by Bizet
Is more Spanish than the Champs Elysées;
We must also admit that every hurdy-gurdy
Owes a deep debt of gratitude
To Guiseppe Verdi. (from 'Not Yet the Dodo')

From *The Wit of Noël Coward* complied by Dick Richards (Leslie Frewin Books Limited, 1970).

R. Morsley Smith

CIVIL SERVANT

Sir,

Your article, 'Will Caruso break a glass for the Advertising Standards Authority' is surely incomplete without reference to Renate Schmetterer, renowned prima donna at the Heidelberg opera at the turn of the century?

Fräulein Schmetterer was so noted for the range and strength of her destructive vocal powers that notices were posted in the foyer whenever she was to perform, advising the audience to leave opera-glasses outside in their carriages. Indeed, the windows of the National Theatre in Berlin had to be heavily shrouded in sacking when she gave *Madame Butterfly* there. On that occasion, by virtue of an injudiciously opened door, the entire bar was brought to liquid ruin.

Although most musical authorities are silent on Fräulein Schmetterer's later exploits, it has become evident from captured Nazi files that, as late as 1944, a scheme was proposed involving her in the role of Sieglinde and a gigantic megaphone on the clifftop at Calais.

[BD: R. Morsley Smith wrote the above to the *New Scientist*. In a letter to me he adds that Fräulein Schmetterer expected and indeed demanded maximum publicity in her day. His great-grandfather was for a short period (about four hours) her English agent and had startling testimony to this.]

Dissatisfied with publicity for her forthcoming concert, the renowned singer strode out into Deansgate, Manchester, on the morning of 16 February 1921 and gave an extempore selection from Richard Strauss's opera *Frau ohne Hemmungen* (dedicated to her). At the last, awesome, *fortissimo* shriek, dozens of motor-cars ground to a halt, their windscreens in smithereens. Traffic signals were shattered; even pavement lights above cellars yielded, depositing passers-by into their depths. The bills for damages were ruinous.

She was married twice – but both marriages broke up. The first was to Adalbert von Trummern and the second to Hugo Schmetterer.

Unusually, both came to an end at the wedding reception. At the first, a green glass epergne, a family heirloom, perished; at the second there was a particularly messy incident during the champagne toast (unhappily performed to music).*

Researches into her Nazi associations have uncovered a hitherto unsuspected complicity in the so-called 'Kristallnacht'!

* BD: Presumably *The Merry Widow*.

Norman Bailey

BASS-BARITONE

No singer can hope to go through his career without something amusingly disastrous happening to him, and I do not seem to be any exception: I have had three so far, all of them connected with my singing Scarpia in *Tosca*.

The first occasion was the one in which I set my wig on fire with the candles at the end of Act II. Fortunately I received only a singeing and not a great conflagration, but there was a distinctly odd smell of burning hanging around the stage for some time afterwards.

The second took place on a very small stage when I was on tour in the provinces in Germany. Scarpia was duly dead, the candles were ceremoniously placed each side of my head, Tosca withdrew from the stage and the curtains closed – leaving (a) my head outside with the audience and (b) my feeling distinctly foolish.

Lastly there was the dress rehearsal of *Tosca* when I sang Scarpia to Anne Evans' Tosca and every actor's inevitable nightmare happened: while chasing Anne around in the attempted rape scene, my trousers fell down!

John Trewin

AUTHOR OF NUMEROUS BOOKS ON THE THEATRE

From time to time for enjoyment I turn back to Alfred Bunn's *The Stage: Both Before and Behind the Curtain* (1840). Bunn was manager of Drury Lane and there on 26 June 1836 Maria Malibran appeared as Isoline in *The Maid of Artois*.

I had occasion during the last rehearsal but one to express myself in strong terms when Malibran left the stage for more than an hour and a half to go and gain £25 at a morning concert. Neither the converted pieces of music, nor the situation of the drama in which she was involved could possibly be proceeded with and the great stake we were contending for was likely to be put in jeopardy by an unworthy grasp at a few pounds to the prejudice of a theatre paying her nightly five times as much.

She knew she had done wrong and atoned for it by her genuis while her pride could not have permitted her to do so. She had borne along the first two acts on the first night of the performance in such a flood of triumph that she was bent by some almost superhuman effort to continue in glory to the final fall of the curtain.

I went into her dressing-room previous to the third act to ask how she felt and she replied: 'Very tired, but . . .' (and here her eye of fire suddenly lighted up) 'you angry devil, if you will contrive to get me a pint of porter in the desert scene, you shall have an encore to your music.' Had I been dealing with any other performer I should perhaps have hesitated in complying with a request that might have been dangerous in its application at the moment; but to check *her* powers was to annihilate them.

I therefore arranged that behind a pile of drifted sand on which she falls in a state of exhaustion towards the close of the desert scene, a small aperture should be made in the stage and it is a fact that from underneath the stage through this aperture a pewter pint of porter was conveyed to the parched lips of this rare child of song, which so revived her after the terrible exertion that the scene led to, that she electrified the audience and had to repeat the charm with the finale to *The Maid of Artois*. The novelty of the circumstances so tickled her fancy and the draught itself was so extremely refreshing that it was arranged during the run of the opera for the negro slave at the head of the Governor's procession to have in the gourd suspended round his neck the same quantity of the same beverage to be applied to her lips on his first beholding the dying Isoline.

During the third act, in the desert of Guiana, the Maid uses the last drop of water to bathe her insensible lover's wounds before breaking into what the *Morning Post* called 'A paroxysm of exultation' that the light is in his eyes again. 'She is in danger of yielding to thirst but fortunately help arrives and everyone is reconciled to everyone else.'

The *Morning Post* added that Malibran gave the finale with 'inexhaustible fire and energy', a 'wondrous burst' that she repeated when the audience demanded it.

Neither the audience nor the *Morning Post* knew about the pewter pints of porter.

Lord Weidenfeld

PUBLISHER

As a small boy of ten I was taken to the opera in Salzburg to see *Der Rosenkavalier* in which Richard Mayr, a friend of my father, was singing Baron Ochs von Lerchenau, a part which he had originated and which Richard Strauss had written for him.

Although it was not my first visit to the opera, I was very excited. I remember, in the intervals, the audience promenaded with their drinks instead of standing at the bar which usually happens these days. I had been given by the lady who looked after me a huge ham sandwich – more like a loaf really – of thick black bread, such as a workman might take with him for his lunch.

As I promenaded with everyone else I became increasingly embarrassed by my ungainly large sandwich – and here was I, in the Salzburg Festival House!

I decided to try to hide it and, hoping to be unnoticed, dropped it on to the carpet. To my horror, it became a centre of attraction. People began to promenade around it as if it were the Golden Calf. My mortification was complete.

However, the story had a happy ending. Richard Mayr, having got to hear of the incident, presented me with a photograph of himself when we met a little later in the Café Bazaar. On it he had written:

> This is for the young man
> who raised more of a furore
> than the opera itself.

Mimi: hot and cold

It was during the Second World War and on a particularly perishingly bitter cold night. The large Scottish auditorium was packed and though there was no heating system working the audience was comfortable enough in overcoats and tammies, flasks and other such self-generated warmth and good cheer.

On-stage it was different – a Siberian waste land with blasts of ice coming from all quarters to discomfort the cast, whose stage costumes gave them no extra protection at all.

The production was *La Bohème* and, of course, the moment came when the tenor sang 'Your tiny hand is frozen'.

And that was the point at which the soprano looked him straight in the eye and in a penetrating whisper which went straight to the back wall of the gods said:

'You're telling Mimi?!'

[BD: Well, I've said all along I'm somewhat doubtful about some of the material in this book.

As it happens, Caruso is on record at the same point in the opera as pressing a hot sausage into Mimi's hand. Mimi was Nellie Melba. Her reaction is not recorded, though it might explain her eager acceptance of an ice-cream pudding being named after her.]

Sir Claus Moser

CHAIRMAN OF THE BOARD OF
DIRECTORS, ROYAL OPERA HOUSE

The thousands of children who regularly lay siege to the Royal Opera House for the special children's matinées have found their own pleasures in these gilded halls.

They slide down the banisters, from Crush Bar to Foyer.

To see the youngsters sliding down always gives me a great sense of pleasure. I have yet to persuade any of the audience on an ordinary night to do it.

George Bernard Shaw

PLAYWRIGHT

A Letter to *The Times*, 3 July 1905

Sir,

The Opera management at Covent Garden regulates the dress of its male patrons. When is it going to do the same to the women?

On Saturday night I went to the Opera. I wore the costume imposed on me by the regulations of the house. I fully recognize the advantage of those regulations. Evening dress is cheap, simple, durable, prevents rivalry and extravagance on the part of male leaders of fashion, annihilates class distinctions, and gives men who are poor and doubtful of their social position (that is, the great majority of men) a sense of security and satisfaction that no clothes of their own choosing could confer, besides saving a whole sex the trouble of considering what they should wear on state occasions. The objections to it are as dust in the balance of the eyes of the ordinary Briton. These objections are that it is colourless and characterless; that it involves a whitening process which makes the shirt troublesome, slightly uncomfortable, and seriously unclean; that it acts as a passport for undesirable persons; that it fails to guarantee sobriety, cleanliness, and order on the part of the wearer; and that it reduces to a formula a very vital human habit which should be the subject of constant experiment and active private enterprise. All such objections are thoroughly un-English. They appeal only to an eccentric few, and may be left out of account with the fantastic objections of men like Ruskin, Tennyson, Carlyle, and Morris to tall hats.

But I submit that what is sauce for the goose is sauce for the gander. Every argument that applies to the regulation of the man's dress applies equally to the regulation of the woman's. Now let me describe what actually happened to me at the opera. Not only was I in evening dress by compulsion, but I voluntarily added many graces of conduct as to which the management made no stipulation whatsoever. I was in my seat for the first chord of the overture. I did not chatter during the music nor raise my voice when the Opera was too loud for normal conversation. I did not get up and go out the moment the Statue music began. My language was fairly moderate considering the number and nature of the improvements on Mozart volunteered by Signor Caruso, and the respectful ignorance of the dramatic points of the score exhibited by the conductor and stage manager – if there is such a functionary at Covent Garden. In short, my behaviour was exemplary.

At 9 o'clock (the Opera began at 8) a lady came in and sat down very conspicuously in my line of sight. She remained there until the beginning of the last act. I do not complain of her coming late and going early; on the contrary, I wish she had come later and gone earlier. For this lady, who had very black hair, had stuck over her right ear the pitiable corpse of a large white bird, which looked exactly as if someone had killed it by stamping on its breast and then nailed it to the lady's temple, which was presumably of sufficient solidity to bear the operation. I am not, I hope a morbidly squeamish person; but the spectacle sickened me. I presume that if I had presented myself at the doors with a dead snake round my neck, a collection of black beetles pinned to my shirtfront, and a grouse in my hair, I should have been refused admission. Why, then, is a woman to be allowed such a public outrage? Had the lady been refused admission, as she should have been, she would have soundly rated the tradesman who imposed the disgusting head-dress on her under the false pretence that 'the best people' wear such things, and withdrawn her custom from him; and thus the root of the evil would be struck at; for your fashionable woman generally allows herself to be dressed according to the taste of a person whom she would not let sit down in her presence. I, once, in Drury Lane, sat behind a matinée hat decorated with the two wings of a seagull, artificially reddened at the joints so as to produce an illusion of being freshly plucked from a live bird. But even that lady stopped short of the whole seagull. Both ladies were evidently regarded by their neighbours as ridiculous and vulgar; but that is hardly enough when the offence is one which produces a sensation of physical sickness in persons of normal humane sensibility.

I suggest to the Covent Garden authorities that, if they feel bound to protect their subscribers against the danger of my shocking them with a blue tie, they are at least equally bound to protect me against the danger of a woman shocking me with a dead bird.

Yours truly,
G. Bernard Shaw

Donald Sinden

ACTOR

A few years ago I decided the time had come to initiate my two sons into the mysteries of an opera house. I chose, in my infinite stupidity, the first night of *Der Rosenkavalier* at Covent Garden with Sena Jurinac as the Marschallin.

Jeremy was sixteen and wore his first dinner jacket. Marc, at twelve, had a black tie appended to a black suit and 'believed' he was wearing a DJ.

Marc perspired glossily throughout the first act until I discovered he was wearing his full set of Chilprufe underwear. In the interval, I was able to remove this in the lavatory – but where could it be hidden . . .? Eventually, my wife secreted it in the arm of her mink jacket.

After the performance, we all went backstage to see some friends and found the dressing-room floors full of evening dresses and DJs – and then, suddenly from the direction of Mme Jurinac's dressing-room a great commotion broke out: 'Send for the manager'; 'Call the fire brigade'; 'Get a mechanic!'

Apparently, on leaving, a visitor to her room had closed the door, and the handle had come off in his hand. The other half had disappeared under a settee. No one could get in and she could not get out. A man charged the door but staggered back with a bruised shoulder.

From my side, the voice of Jeremy rang out, newly-broken and with great authority: 'Stand back, everyone!'

An avenue opened and he advanced on the door. Now who else in that elegant throng would be likely to be carrying a massive penknife in his pocket containing tools for every emergency?

Deftly, he unscrewed the lock and released the captive. Not to be outdone, Marc shot into the room, bowed to Mme Jurinac and said: 'May I present you to your rescuer?'

She was enchanted and duly signed their programmes with suitable inscriptions of gratitude.

Arthur Marshall

JOURNALIST

The modern language and music staffs, hot for culture, combined to press for the showing of a German silent film of *Der Ring des Nibelungen* with English sub-titles (to help explain the unfolding action) such as: 'Brünnhilde in Siegfried's arms is all woman'.

To add to the excitement, Wagnerian themes galore were thundered out on the school organ. All went well until Siegfried, a blond beast quite spent after making swords and cleaving anvils and leaping about after his bride-to-be, decided to take a refreshing dip in a studio pool conveniently to hand. Swiftly discarding various items of equipment, mangey furs, those frightful cross-garterings and kicking off his sandals, he peeled off his tunic and treated us, not to a full-frontal, but a full rear-view of a vast German bottom wobbling its way beneath the healing waters.

At this point, the music having momentarily stopped, I and certain other members of the house I was in, feeling that something was needed, applauded.

Fatal mistake, as it turned out, and we got a fearful wigging from the housemaster ('You have blackened our faces in public').

So much for trying to help things along.

From an article in the *New Statesman*, 12 May 1978.

Warren Brown

FORMER STORY EDITOR, MGM

At an open-air performance of *Carmen* in Chicago the 'curtain' to allow the stage to be cleared at the end of each act was replaced by a powerful array of floodlights which were supposed to dazzle the audience momentarily.

Throughout the performance, the Don José was so lyrically infatuated with himself that neither Carmen (Gladys Swarthout) nor Michaela was able to divert him from his up-stage posturing. Not altogether surprisingly, Carmen switched her enthusiasm to Escamillo with a rapidity not altogether called for in the libretto.

When the moment came for Don José to stab Carmen, he did so with such relish that the audience gasped. She fell and struck the boards violently and lay as though truly dead. The opera ended fittingly with José's arrest. The audience was dazzled by the flashing floods but when it came time for the curtain calls Gladys Swarthout was still unconscious and had to be propped up by Michaela and Escamillo.

Next day she told reporters that she was not injured '. . . just terribly, terribly hurt'.

That particular Don José, in fact, had a considerable reputation for one-man performances in practically every opera he was cast in. *La Bohème* was no exception, where he sang Rodolfo opposite Grace Moore as Mimi.

'I had for several years', she said, 'at various opera houses, given performances of *Bohème* with that man and inevitably, at every performance, just before I made my first entrance, exhausted and fainting, I would find that he had carefully turned the chair into which I weakly lower myself so that it faced up-stage.

'Tired of having to sing my opening aria with my back to the conductor and the audience, I devised a little plan. At that evening's performance, I made my first entrance to find Rodolfo struggling furiously with the chair – which refused to budge.

'I sat, facing the audience for the first time that season, allowing myself just a little private smile of satisfaction. Rodolpho, for his part, only gave up the battle to turn me round when the script demanded he held my hand to note how cold it was.

'I felt the dollar or so I had paid the stage crew to nail the chair to the floor had been well spent.'

The Countess of Harewood

FORMER VIOLINIST

I remember a performance of *Tosca* in Buenos Aires where, at the end of the second act, the stage director suddenly recalled that he had a new bunch of extras on that evening. He had not explained to them what they were to do once they were dressed as soldiers in the last act.

He rushed backstage a few moments before the curtain was due to go up on the last act, herded them together and then, pointing to the evening's prima donna, issued the injunction:

'When the stage manager gives you the signal, follow that woman.'

They did. Even to the extent of jumping after her, lemming-like, over the battlements.

[BD: In the face of apparently overwhelming factual reports of sightings I remain slightly sceptical about the stories of the Toscas who, having hurled themselves the necessary half mile or so to the Tiber, immediately bounce back into public gaze. Vilem Tausky

53

swears it happened to Joan Hammond at Covent Garden: Joan Hammond was not available for comment. A member of the audience at the Puccini Theatre in Bari, Southern Italy, around the end of the Second World War, alleges he saw it happen. The airborne Tosca was Anna Farone. 'I can only assume that opera houses all over the world later borrowed the Bari landing-strip,' he says.]

J. J. Maling

AUTHOR

In the mid-1940s the newly re-formed Bari opera did a one-night stand each week at the Fenice Cinema at Molfetta, a little town a few miles up the coast from Bari. Their star singer was Mino Cavallo, a singer of some standing who had a reputation for remaining calm – no matter what.

For *Rigoletto* at the cinema the stage was divided for Act i Scene ii by the usual wall down the centre, one side lit for Rigoletto's house, the other left dark as the street. In a moment of high passion, Cavallo staggered so dramatically against the wall that it gave way. He was not a man to be put off by such a piffling happening and, still singing, grabbed it before it fell. At the same time he signalled to the conductor, Dino Milella, for help. Without missing a beat, Milella despatched one of his string players to creep out of the pit to find the stage carpenter.

Sure enough, shortly afterwards, a man in overalls crawled on all fours on to the dark part of the stage with a piece of wood and a bag of tools. Reaching the wall, he sat down, clattered about in his bag and took out a thick six-inch nail.

The opera continued with the audience's attention now divided between Rigoletto and the new 'character'. The carpenter, having put his piece of wood in place to his satisfaction, paused, hammer in hand, debating whether to try to do the job quietly or to have one almighty swipe to get it over with.

He went for a quick finish. Rigoletto, still propping up the wall and still singing, didn't even flinch as an inch or so of pointed steel appeared slightly above his hand.

The carpenter, dropping again to hands and knees, crawled off to a round of applause from the audience.

To round off the story of the fortunes of the Molfetta cinema, its last production was *La Forza del Destino* which never finished. The lights failed.

They didn't come on again for two weeks.

Not anywhere in the town.

Sir Charles Mackerras

CONDUCTOR AND COMPOSER

I was conducting Gounod's *Faust* with the Dublin Grand Opera Society, where the scenery tended to be rough and ready.

At the end of the garden scene when Marguerite opens her window to sing of her love for Faust, the window stuck and wouldn't move at all. As it didn't have any glass in it, the soprano was able to continue singing, even through an apparently closed window.

An over-keen stage-hand, seeing the problem, tried to creep up behind the flat and open the window for her.

Unfortunately, in the dark, his hand lost its way and went up Marguerite's skirt. Instead of the window opening, all we saw was the lady's skirt rising and her hand slapping down some unseen object below.

Sir Geraint Evans

INTERNATIONAL STAR BARITONE

One of the funniest things that happened to me was in self-defence in an early television production of *Carmen* in the days when everything had to go out 'live' because there was no pre-recording. One shot the producer was particularly fond of was of me swaggering into the tavern in Act II to stand under an electric fan in the ceiling. It was all right at rehearsals because the fan was not switched on. During transmission, it was going full blast.

I duly swaggered in, took up my stance – and realized that the up-draught was taking my wig with it. It was literally rising off my head. I knew I was on camera from the waist up only, so I did the only thing I could – I pretended to walk down two imaginary steps with the result that the viewers saw me lose two feet in height in as many seconds and I had to carry on singing with my knees bent.

Michael Langdon and I occasionally break out (off-stage this is) in pulling gags on each other and I remember on one such occasion in Los Angeles we were fooling around with our raincoat collars pulled up over our ears playing cops. I 'shot' Michael at the top of a flight of stairs and he staggered down clutching the wall with an entirely realistic 'Aaaggghhh'! What he didn't know was that I hadn't followed him down. Somebody else had – a complete stranger of whom Michael, to his extreme embarrassment, suddenly caught sight. Straightening up, the only thing he could think of to say was, 'Sorry about that. I think I must have twisted my ankle or something.'

I saw someone else in a much more embarrassing predicament on-stage in San Francisco – a soprano singing the Marschallin in

Der Rosenkavalier. She had two white Pekinese dogs in a basket, one of which she picked up and placed on her lap. The excitement was too much for the creature who promptly answered a call of nature right down the front of her dress. The poor woman sat there in the full knowledge that a ten-minute aria was coming up for her any minute.

Here in London, in *La Bohème*, I was playing Schaunard. In the last act when I challenge Colline to a mock duel, I fended off his sword with an old cushion which suddenly collapsed. You couldn't see us for feathers and the orchestra were still picking them out of their instruments at the end of the evening.

Kenneth Vincent Masterton

FORMERLY MANCHESTER OPERA HOUSE

[BD: For the technically-minded only; otherwise, take it slowly.]

As a newly demobbed airman I took a job as a flyman at the Manchester Opera House just at a time when Covent Garden moved in on a one-week stand on a nation-wide tour. The opening production was *Il Trovatore*. We worked solidly for forty-eight hours getting in the sets. In the flies we had a 'hanging plot' but no 'flying plot' and were dependent on the Garden men for cueing.

So. Came the first night. The house lights had gone, the curtain was up and Act I was away – castle wall exterior cloth in downstage, cut to take a portcullis. The Captain of the Guard strode on rousing the soldiers from sleep in order to deliver to the audience the all-important 'new readers begin here' aria.

The cue (Q1) to the flies was 'take out portcullis slowly'. In reality Q1 caused utter panic up above, and up came the castle wall at high speed, leaving the portcullis on-stage on its own with the soldiers bewildered but bravely singing still and marching round and round it. We in the flies decided to try to put the matter right and dropped in the castle wall more quickly, if anything, than the speed with which we had taken it out.

Q2 to the flies was 'take out the castle wall at high speed . . .' and away went the portcullis at high speed. The cast was by now totally confused, singing inside and outside the castle wall. Finally we got the lot out. Despite this desperate confusion no one in the audience commented on the chaos.

Next evening was *The Magic Flute* with the American soprano Doris Dorée singing the Queen of the Night. Her costume was black, the setting was dark and Miss Dorée was standing on an eight feet high rostrum. The only lighting was a pin spot on her face. She herself could see very little and all the audience saw was a face apparently floating about thirteen feet in the air.

In striking the preceding scene I had flown out another cut cloth and I was unaware that it had fouled another hanging piece which, during the course of the Queen of the Night's scene, was slowly tilting towards one side. This was caused by the bottom weight (a 'tumbler' in the trade) slowly slipping out of its turn-up ('sleeve'). In this case the weight was a piece of wood about fifteen feet long and eight inches in diameter. Eventually the cloth tilted far enough for the wood to slide out – as, indeed, it did – and shot like a spear on to the stage floor fifty feet below.

There was a terrible thud as it hit the boards, then a clatter as it fell into the wings.

The Queen of the Night stopped singing, the music stopped – until the conductor took firm hold again and we were back with *The Magic Flute* as written.

The odd thing was that the next day a national newspaper carried a headline 'SINGER NARROWLY MISSES DEATH'.

As far as I know the only person who was hit was a stage-hand. The tumbler landed near him but he simply picked it up and propped it in a corner. It was used afterwards as a clearing stick.

It'll be all right on the night

An ambitious London opera group's production of *Faust* introduced the heavenly intervention to rescue Marguerite's soul from Mephistophiles by shattering the gloom of the prison by opening a set of tabs on a rostrum upstage. A broad shaft of brilliant blue light on to the stage was to reveal a line-up of eight members of the chorus dressed as mediaeval angels in blue and gold robes, each flourishing a long trumpet.

On the night, the angels were assembled when one of them noticed something odd about one of her colleagues: he was completely blue, no gold anywhere.

He had put his costume on back to front. (The audience would see only the front so there was no point in wasting gold trimming.)

Her gasp of dismay drew the attention of the rest of the chorus to the luckless tenor and with only sixty seconds to go before the tabs were due to open, the rest made a concerted grab at him. He protested and struggled until with only seconds to spare, they had switched his costume round and dived for their tableau positions.

As it was, they could hardly keep their faces straight imagining what had so nearly happened: the curtains opening to reveal a gang of angels stripping the one in the middle.

An elementary opera put on by small children again featured angels. Having gone off from the prompt side, they were due to return OP when the Evil One (adult) having supposedly sighted them, declared: 'Aha! Here come the Forces of the Enemy', cupping his hand to his ear to emphasize the point. It was all right during rehearsals, but, on the night, the performance took place not on the school stage, which they all knew, but in a local hall.

The Evil One duly said his line in his listening attitude.
Nothing happened.
He said the words again.
Still no result.

With a presence of mind which impressed even him when he thought about it later, he remembered that there was no way round the back of the stage as there was at school. So. He strode across to the Prompt Side where the angel band had last been seen and cried: 'Aha! Here they come! The Forces of the Enemy!'

Again, nothing happened . . . except that the audience began to titter because there began to trickle on OP a most disreputable, dirty and disintegrating band of quite definitely fallen angels, wings bent, haloes askew, dresses, arms and legs filthy.

The producer had made them all crawl under the stage so as to be able to enter from the correct side, as rehearsed.

A company based in the North of England reckon that an evening spent in their local pub after one of their rehearsals would have filled this book. [BD: From their account, I believe them.]

In their *Faust*, for instance, in the drinking scene, the wine duly flowed from the wall when it should – but wouldn't stop. Time after time, the men in the chorus rushed up to the spouting Bacchus to refill their mugs with foul-tasting pink water in order to stop the stage becoming awash. This went on for about fifteen minutes while the stage staff rushed around trying to turn back the tide. They never found the cause ... it is alleged.

In *La Forza del Destino* the chorus amassed in the wings ready for what they refer to as 'the rush on'. Norah, pride of the society at four feet six inches, failed to recognize the cue, so someone gave her a hefty shove – and out shot both sets of her false teeth. They clattered out on to the stage followed by 'a tittering bunch of hooligans' [BD: not my description].

The scene finished with a gauze drop behind which the chorus knelt for 'an aria or two' during which time everybody scrabbled around in semi-darkness trying to find Norah's teeth. In the event, she had to finish the act without them.

On another occasion they reckon they were all offered walk-on parts in *William Tell* at Sadler's Wells, the company being invited *en bloc*. As most of them had daytime jobs their trip to London had to be fitted in as best it could. Most people miscalculated the length of the journey. The result was, as some of them also had difficulty in finding the theatre, the curtain went up 'on a rousing chorus of one man carrying a sports bag and two women in full costume'. As the act progressed, more people arrived to populate the stage in various stages of make-up and costume. The principals, whom the group had never met, were completely baffled 'but had a good laugh afterwards'.

This same company has in its time also had to undergo such ordeals as Marguerita's flowers being nailed to the floor (by accident, of course), Carmen's entry at the top of a flight of stairs being thwarted because there weren't any steps down (so she stood, marooned for the rest of the act) and soldiers' hats failing to turn up on time which led to the men having to go on in buckets, specially painted for the occasion.

[BD: I can't vouch for any of this – but *name and address* were supplied.]

63

Dame Bridget D'Oyly Carte

MANAGING DIRECTOR, D'OYLY CARTE COMPANY

I remember particularly one performance of *The Yeomen of the Guard*. The supers, not members of the company, having been told to clear the stage on the cue 'clear the rabble' nearly provoked an on-stage fight as they tried to shove off Jack Point – the principal comedian – along with the rest of the chorus.

Michael Kilgarrif

ACTOR AND AUTHOR

Rutland Barrington, originator of many of the comic roles in the Savoy operas, was heavily built. During one of the rehearsals for *HMS Pinafore* he was asked by Gilbert to cross the stage and sit down on a property sky-light 'pensively'. Barrington did as he was told but his bulk was too much for the flimsy prop which immediately collapsed underneath him.

'Oh for goodness' sake, Barrington,' sighed Gilbert, surveying the wreckage, 'I said "pensively" not "expensively".'

Barrington, for all his comedy success, was never a particularly good singer. At the first night of *Patience* Gilbert was sitting watching him from his stage box with a group of friends.

'Barrington's in good voice,' one of them said. 'He's singing in tune!'

'Yes,' replied Gilbert. 'First night nerves.'

Gilbert's tongue got the better of him in New York where he was being deeply bored by an insistent woman at a party trying to impress him with her deep love and knowledge of music.

'I do so admire Mr Bach's music,' she gushed. 'Tell me, is he still composing?'

'No, madam,' said Gilbert, hardly believing his luck – 'decomposing.'

From *Best Showbiz Jokes* by Michael Kilgarrif (Woolfe Publishing Limited, 1974).

W. S. Gilbert on cue

[BD: There seems to be a limitless supply of Gilbert's well-honed witticisms. . . .]

Asked if he had seen much of Mrs So-and-so lately Gilbert replied, 'No, not much. Only her face and hands.'

A fellow member of the Garrick Club asked Gilbert, 'Have you seen a man here with one eye called Green?'
  'No,' came the answer. 'What's the name of his other eye?'

An Australian wrote to Gilbert suggesting they collaborated and explaining that he was 'a chemist by profession and a born musician'.
  Gilbert replied, 'I should have preferred to have collaborated with you had you been born a chemist and a musician by profession.'

Peggy Ann Jones

SOPRANO

One night I was playing Phoebe in *The Yeomen of the Guard*. The spinning wheel I had was a small compact job but incredibly old, and it collapsed under me as I was trying to hold it together. You have no idea how many pieces of wood go into making a spinning wheel. And as each piece fell off, I was madly trying to remember the words, sing the song, and look as if this happened every night. I ended up with a heap of wood on the floor – and then had to pick up all the pieces and stomp off with them.

One last night of a London season – I swear this is an accident – in *Patience* I was supposed to sing:

> But who is this whose god-like grace
> Proclaims he comes from noble race

But for some inexplicable reason, I sang:

> But who is this of god-like grace
> Proclaims he comes from Outer Space

The whole company collapsed. Ken Sandford came on and wondered what everyone was laughing at. He thought his flies were undone.

Elastic is constantly going. It happened to me once on *The Gondoliers*. We had pantaloons plus a petticoat and when I ran on-stage I tripped and fell flat on my face and was terribly embarrassed. Then I felt the elastic going. I was skipping round in a big circle with someone holding each of my hands so I couldn't do a thing about it. The pants finished up round my ankles so that I couldn't move properly. I was by now completely oblivious of the audience, wondering how to get these things off my legs. Eventually I stood on one leg and then the other, pulling off the pantaloons as best I could. I kicked them into the wings – and with them went one shoe. The audience fell about. It was the biggest laugh of the night. I was mortified.

Beti Lloyd-Jones

CONTRALTO

My drawers dropped down in *The Pirates of Penzance* when we opened in Bristol. [BD: No comment.]

I think one of the funniest things, though, for the other members of the company – it wasn't funny for me at the time – is that I started to sing Inez an octave too high.

Inez starts in middle C and works up to the D above C, and I started too high. It was desperate, terrible. I didn't know what to do because I'm essentially a contralto and would have finished up on D in alto had I continued. Fortunately, I had the common sense to talk the middle part of it and managed to catch the note from the orchestra to finish in the right key.

I was the only person on the stage who didn't laugh. I bawled my head off in the dressing-room. I just couldn't believe it. I don't know whether I hadn't concentrated. I heard the note from the orchestra. I just started off suddenly and kept going up and up and I thought 'Well, I can't go any further' so I just had to talk it. The Musical Director could see the whites of my eyes as I got higher and higher. It was ridiculous. I think it's the worst thing that has ever happened to me.

Tommy Steele

ENTERTAINER

I had one experience in *The Yeomen of the Guard* which was, of course, my first real contact with the world of opera, when it was given in the open air at the Tower of London a couple of years back and I sang Jack Point.

About three days before the opening, I was told to meet the company at the 'sitzprobe' (I am not sure how to spell this word, let alone pronounce it, or what it means).

I asked where it was and was told it would be within the precincts of the Tower. So I went there and combed every tea bar, restaurant, pub, etc. in the neighbourhood until I eventually ended up near Traitors' Gate.

And that was where – at a distance – I began to hear the sound of an orchestra. I ran towards it – and there was the full company and orchestra rehearsing. Everyone except me, that is.

In my world, I think a sitzprobe might be called a band-call.

[BD: I don't know whether I can spell 'sitzprobe' either but Colin Busby of the London Philharmonic Orchestra, who regularly plays at Glyndebourne, tells me that in an opera house a sitzprobe happens very early on in a new production with the singers on stage with notebooks but *no* director. The iron is usually down so there is no direct contact between singers and musicians (which can either be the whole orchestra or one piano). The idea is for the singers to 'breathe' themselves into the words before the director takes over to give moves, etc.]

John Culshaw

AUTHOR AND PRODUCER

I like the story of the days when the D'Oyly Carte company used to tour the provinces week by week with only a nucleus of principal orchestral musicians, since it was possible to pick up the rank and file players in each location.

One such was the second oboe, who was therefore always one of the new faces at the beginning of each week. There was only one conductor at the time and he was not universally popular. He was also understandably nervous because, wherever he went, he encountered what was virtually a new orchestra every Monday night.

In the orchestral part provided for the 'local' second oboe there was an instruction written against a certain note about half-way through the work. It said:

'Play B flat on Wednesday matinées *only*. It drives him bloody mad!'

Beecham on Beecham

There is in every large town of every country at least one individual who is the living terror of managers, conductors, pianists, and every other kind of artist. This is the single-composer enthusiast. For this type of fanatic no other music at all except that of the object of his idolatry exists. If he thinks his idol is being insufficiently played he writes long and frequent letters to the press. He attends all concerts where any composition of the master is being given, and if there is something in the performance he does not like, he fires off a volley of oral or epistolary abuse at the misguided or incompetent interpreter. He is always *plus royaliste que le roi* and there is no escape from him; in other words, he is the world's greatest bore and number one nuisance.

I have already suffered the attentions of the leading Strauss devotee and watchdog in London, so I was hardly surprised when he got in touch with me over *Elektra*:

Sir:

Do you intend to imitate the cheeseparing habits of the Grand Opera Syndicate? What's coming over you? Last night from my coign of vantage in the gallery, I counted your orchestra and could discover no more than ninety-eight players. As you well know, Strauss has stipulated for no less than one hundred and eleven. What have you done with the rest? Please answer at once.

Yours anxiously ...

For the moment I felt like the unhappy Varius when the Emperor Augustus confronted him with the terrifying demand:
'*Where* are my legions?'

I thought I might quite easily have lost a few of my men without noticing it, and a favourite criticism of the malicious was that I could have dispensed with a great many without the ordinary ear being able to discern the difference. Surely it was impossible for a company of them to have trooped out while I was conducting without my noticing?

To satisfy myself, I went up to the exalted spot which 'Yours anxiously' had termed his 'coign of vantage' and discovered the explanation of the mystery. From there it was impossible to see the full orchestra, some of them having been concealed in and under boxes, and so, greatly relieved, I was able to send a reply that all was well and the temple had not been profaned.

As my advisers were strongly of the opinion that my first important season should be given at Covent Garden, there I went.

The programme was made up of *Elektra, A Village Romeo and Juliet, Ivanhoe, Tristan and Isolde, The Wreckers, Carmen, Hansel and Gretel* and *L'Enfant Prodigue*. With the exception of *Elektra* none of the other novelties and unfamiliar pieces met with popular success, although the general attendance was pretty good.

A Village Romeo and Juliet was pronounced as 'undramatic' by the press, although I myself have never been able to discover the deficiency of it. All the same Delius has certainly a method of writing opera shared by no one else. So long as the singers are off the stage, the orchestra plays delicately and enchantingly, but the moment they reappear, it strikes up fiercely and complainingly as if it resented not being allowed to relate the whole story by itself.

During the last act the curtain is down for about eight minutes and the orchestra plays a strain of haunting beauty – an intermezzo now known to every concert-goer as 'The Walk to the Paradise Garden'. But in the theatre it went for next to nothing, being almost completely drowned by the conflicting sounds of British workmen battering on the stage and the loud conversation of the audience.

When I revived the work some time later I introduced here a new stage picture, so that this lovely piece was played with the curtain up – the only way in an English theatre to secure comparative silence. What the public does not see, it takes no interest in, and I would advise all young composers, if they wish their music to be heard, never to lower the curtain for one second during the course

Lucy.

of an act. Better let it remain up with the operations of scene shifting and workmen in shirt sleeves in full view: possibly a fair proportion of the spectators will go away afterwards under the impression that these were part of the entertainment.

[BD: That Sir Thomas was absolutely correct was proved recently by Timothy West playing in *Beecham* at the Apollo Theatre. The curtain was lowered for the interval, 'Walk to the Paradise Garden' was played – and the audience chatted away merrily, in complete oblivion.]

From a broadcast by Sir Thomas Beecham:
You know, I must confess to a weakness which very few English musicians would confess to – I really like music. There is no end of fun to be derived from it, especially in an opera house when you are running it yourself. I was for over thirty years involved off and on running opera houses here and there and hardly a day passed without some side-splitting imbecility.

I always remember poor Chaliapin who was rehearsing the last act of *Don Quixote* where there is a trio. He would never sing with the other two in rehearsal and it was very untidy – so I complained.

All at once the Dulcinea appeared from the cornice and said:

'Sir! I cannot!'

'Cannot what?'

'I cannot. Monsieur Chaliapin, he always dies too soon.'

I said:

'Madam. You are in error. No operatic artist ever dies half soon enough for me!'

The BBC once caught a blast from Sir Thomas by offering £15 (in 1951) for permission to broadcast his arrangement of Michael Balfe's *The Bohemian Girl*.

'That arrangement', Sir Thomas wrote in reply, 'has involved the thought of twenty-five years ... at no time and nowhere in the course of a long career have I received such a preposterously inadequate, thoroughly impudent and magnificently inept proposal from anyone.'

Singed by this frontal attack the BBC made another offer. The work was broadcast. No further details became known.

When Sir Thomas brought *Die Meistersinger* back to London the staff of the Royal Opera House felt some honour was needed for the occasion and lined themselves up in an informal committee of welcome, front of house. Somehow Sir Thomas had word in advance of what was to happen and with his well-known sense of fun arrived unannounced by the stage door.

Once inside the theatre he went down to the pit, took off his jacket – and the first thing the reception committee knew of his arrival was hearing the tremendous C major chord with which the opera begins.

The previous day someone had telephoned him to say that he was on the point of sending round a score 'marked with the cuts'.

'Marked with the *what*?' demanded Sir Thomas.

Silence.

'How many people are there in the chorus?'

'—er, about sixty, I think, Sir Thomas—'

'Sixty? Sixty! I had one hundred and fifty before the war. And I'd like to have them now. And the opera will be sung in full. And, what's more, in German!'

From Norman Morrison, member of the Sir Thomas Beecham Society.

Sir Neville Cardus

CRITIC

He [Beecham] could be naughty. He twice withdrew my tickets from Covent Garden because he didn't approve of my reviews. In one of them, I pointed out that he had ruined an otherwise superb performance of *Siegfried* by a reckless speedway tempo in the closing act. Next morning, he rang me saying, 'I see from today's *Guardian* that you have been even more fatuous than usual. You write that I ruined the last act by a reckless tempo.'

'So you did,' I replied.

'You critics,' he responded, 'are very inhumane. My orchestra had been in the pit since five-thirty on a hot summer night. At the beginning of the last act, I took note of the time – after ten o'clock. And the pubs close at eleven. My orchestra had not had a drink for hours. And many of the dear people in the audience had to get back home to Woking and Pinner.'

'So I said to my orchestra – Whoops . . .!'

Incorrigible.

His geniality was the sugar for the pill of his tongue. During an interval at an opera rehearsal, one of the singers asked for his advice:

'I've just got a son come down from Oxford. What do you think I should persuade him to go in for? He doesn't fancy law or politics. And I don't want him to waste himself in any business job.'

'Why not make a singer of him?' Sir Thomas enquired blandly.

'Oh no. He hasn't any particular kind of voice,' explained the singer.

'Ah. I see,' came the reply – 'a family failing!'

From an article in the 25th Anniversary Booklet of the Royal Philharmonic Orchestra.

Victor Borge

ENTERTAINER, MUSICIAN AND WIT

Everybody knows that *Carmen* is one of the most glorious operas ever written. Nobody knew it when Bizet was around to enjoy it but as soon as he died they knew it right away. That's the way things always happened to him. First of all the story had to be completely redone because in the original version by Prosper Mérimée, Don José is really Lizzarrabengoa of Elizondo, and Escamillo, the toreador, is really a picador named Lucas, and Carmen is really carrying on with Garcia the One-Eyed, and there isn't a single girl called Micaëla at all.

When the plot was finally straightened out, Bizet heaved a sigh of relief and turned to the music. Don't ask. To begin with, he had to compose the whole opera in his madhouse of an apartment, with his baby screaming, balloons popping, and the man upstairs giving piano lessons all day long. Bizet would wrap a big scarf around his head to shut out the clatter, but students would come by asking for advice and publishers would pester him for pieces he hadn't gotten quite around to composing yet. Also clomping around the place was the maid's eleven-year-old son. (Nobody knew for sure who the kid's father was. It could be a coincidence that Bizet had come home for a visit exactly nine months before he was born.)

Long before the score was finished, the Directors of the Opera House decided to take a look at it. They nearly had a fit. For one thing, their theatre was a favourite spot for marriage brokers, for here their prospective clients were introduced to each other, and a sexy seductress like Carmen could ruin the wedding business for months to come. They were even more upset at having an unhappy ending, and they were positively hysterical when they realized there would actually be a murder on stage. Bizet patiently

76

explained that it would be a teeny little murder, and he promised to sneak it in next to a ballet and a parade and stuff so that nobody would notice. He also agreed to cut a few passionate scenes with Carmen's husband, who was a pickpocket in the original story, but that's as far as he would go. (In fact, he threw the whole pickpocketing husband right out of the opera.)

The next problem was to find a singer to create the title role. The first candidate mentioned in the newspapers was a café entertainer named Zelma Bouffar, but she considered it touffar beneath her dignity to be stabbed in the finale and turned it down. Then the part was offered to an operetta star called Marie Roze, but she sank to the occasion and declined because the story was too immoral. That left Marie Célestine Laurence Galli-Marié, whose dignity and morals were more flexible. Bizet played his music for her, got her home address, just in case, and told the director of the Opera that he had found his Carmen at last.

He had. But from now on the Director haggled endlessly with Galli-Marié over salary and vacations, until she wrote a sarcastic letter to a friend, referring to the director as a monkey. That would not have been so bad had she not mailed it to the Opera House by mistake, and guess who was opening the letters that day? For months, Bizet was exasperated, convinced that the whole project was collapsing. It wasn't, though, and in the fall of 1874, Galli-Marié arrived in Paris to begin preparations for the première of *Carmen*.

What happened before was just fun and games compared to the chaos of the rehearsals. Before Bizet could count to anything everybody tried to get in on the first act. The men in the orchestra complained that their parts were unplayable, and the chorus threatened to go on strike because Bizet wanted them to move around in the crowd scenes, instead of just standing there staring at the conductor. Later, the women in the chorus made Bizet rewrite one of the big ensemble numbers because it was too difficult. And, since the librettists usually had better things to do than attending rehearsals with everybody screaming at everybody else, the composer even had to rewrite some of the lyrics.

As the battle with the chorus simmered down, Galli-Marié decided that she didn't like her entrance number and she made Bizet rework it at least a dozen times. When she announced she didn't much care for version thirteen either, Bizet got disgusted, went to the library, dragged out a book of Spanish folk songs, swiped one of the tunes and wrote 'Habanera' across the top in big letters. Well, no sooner was Carmen settled than out ran Escamillo, yelling that he didn't like his entrance number either. This time Bizet was ready. He went to the library and dragged out the book of Spanish folk songs straight away. But he couldn't find any more good tunes, so he plunked himself down at a table and dashed off the 'Toreador Song'. 'If they want garbage, they'll get garbage,' he grumbled, which just shows how little Bizet knew about writing popular operas. (He didn't actually use the word 'garbage', but I'd just as soon not go into the matter any further, if you don't mind.)

Carmen had an unhappy ending in more ways than one. Only two or three of Bizet's friends were good enough liars to pretend the opera was a success. The rest slunk quietly away and the composer wandered the streets half the night in deep despair. After a while he began to feel a little better.

Then the reviews came out. 'Bizet's music is painful, noisy, blatant and eminently repulsive,' said one of the kinder critics. 'If the devil were to write an opera,' said another, 'it would come out sounding very much like *Carmen*.' Bizet's masterpiece struggled along for several months, but the theatre was half-empty and the receipts from the ticket sales did not even cover production costs.

Today, naturally, we know that Bizet's critics were wrong. Even they came to know it because, within a very few years (alas, after Bizet had died at the age of thirty-seven) *Carmen* became the most fantastic success in the annals of opera. It was staged in Brazil and Latvia and Australia and Norway and America. Brahms went to see it twenty times. It was given in Japanese and Estonian and Danish and Swedish and Hebrew and Slovenian and Chinese and Portuguese and Bulgarian. In Russia it was a tremendous hit as *Carmencita and the Soldier* and in Spain they presented it in a bull ring. Yes they did. They hired a real toreador and a real bull and had a real bull fight in the middle of the opera.

As the years went by, *Carmen* became more and more popular. It was staged well over three thousand times at the Opéra-Comique alone, and when the lofty Paris Opéra decided to give it a brand new production, they fixed it up with horses, dogs, donkeys, monkeys and (in the audience) General de Gaulle. We've had movie *Carmens* and jazz *Carmens* and rock *Carmens* and ballet *Carmens*. There was a *Carmen* at the Metropolitan Opera House in New York starring Beatrice Lillie in a kilt. A Russian composer has done a version using forty-seven percussion instruments and an American concocted one for solo kazoo and symphony orchestra. We've seen *Carmen Jones* with an all-black cast and *The Naked Carmen* with, never mind.

You know something? Maybe Georges Bizet wasn't so unlucky after all. The only version of *Carmen* he ever knew was the original, the one that has come to be called 'the queen of operas'.

From *My Favourite Intermissions* by Victor Borge (Doubleday and Company, 1971).

Vilem Tausky

CONDUCTOR

When I was a young conductor, about twenty at the time, I was working in the Opera House at Brno. One day I happened to be in the office of the administrative director, Jiři Jiřikovský, a man with a great sense of humour, when his secretary, Dr Leoš Firkušný (brother of Rudolph Firkušný) appeared.

'Pani Žaludová is here to see you,' he said, 'in a filthy temper because her dates have been altered!'

I got up hastily to leave but Jiřikovský said, 'Stay here, young man; you may have something to learn to your advantage.'

I sat down – reluctantly. And in stormed the prima donna.

'What,' she demanded, 'is the meaning of this injustice? My dates were fixed months ago and I have made my arrangements accordingly. Who is this Russian woman that her convenience should be studied over mine?'

On and on she went and Jiřikovský listened silently.

But gradually his eye brightened. Slowly, he rose and walked towards her.

'Tell me,' he said, 'is that a new outfit you are wearing? I don't think I've seen you in it before. The colour is so becoming. And that hat! It's *so* right with the whole ensemble.'

'Do you really think so?' asked Žaludová. 'I am so glad you like it. The hat was my own idea. . . .'

The tantrums subsided. The dates were subtly adjusted.

As the door closed on Pani Žaludová, the director said to me with a wink:

'Let that be a lesson to you for life, young man!'

Ian Wallace

OPERA SINGER AND BROADCASTER

It was the last act of *La Bohème* at the Cambridge Theatre, London. Mimi lay dying and the four friends in the attic were wondering what to do.

Before Colline took out his overcoat to pawn he came over to Schaunard, who was standing near the table on which was a spirit lamp, to tell him tactfully to withdraw and leave Rudolfo and Mimi alone, Marcel having gone off with Musetta to find a doctor.

Alexandre Benois had designed this production and Colline wore an old tail coat with two large buttons at the back. He leaned against the table while singing to Schaunard and by some miracle of mischance the spirit lamp got hooked on to one of the buttons on the back of his coat and as he turned to leave the stage he had acquired a tail-light.

I was playing Schaunard and had to follow him out pretty closely to avoid the audience seeing this ludicrous sight at such a sad moment. Marion Nowakowski, who was Colline, had no idea what had happened until I unhooked the lamp and asked him what the hell he thought he was playing at! He couldn't believe his eyes.

Now it was essential to get the lamp back on-stage to warm Mimi's medicine. I was first to re-enter so had to take it on concealed in my jacket, making a mysterious circle of the table to 'palm' it back on.

It is at moments like that that hysteria is very near and I was lucky that my shaking shoulders were interpreted by the audience as paroxysms of grief.

Steve Race

BROADCASTER

I cannot claim to have any personal experience of opera production but I have had contacts (usually very agreeable ones) with opera stars over the years, notably Ian Wallace and the late David Franklin in the radio and television series 'My Music'.

For example, I remember asking David a question about *Rigoletto*.

'As the heroine is dying, Rigoletto's final line is sung very loudly', I pointed out. 'Why so loudly at such a tender moment?'

'Probably', observed David, 'because the orchestra is playing so loudly!' (Actually, of course, Rigoletto is calling out that the curse of Count Monterone has been fulfilled.)

At that point Ian Wallace recalled that an Italian soprano once played the part of Gilda despite the fact that she was (in his words) 'a very big girl indeed'. After being murdered, she has to be carried off in her sack by Sparafucile. The poor singer playing Sparafucile found himself utterly unable to shift the sack once she was in it, so for the performance in which the lady took part, it was arranged that Sparafucile should have three burly brothers who came on at that point in the story to help him with his burden! In spite of this, on some nights even the four of them could not manage her, and then the audience would see two little legs poking out of the sack, twinkling along by way of help.

David remembered having similar trouble with a well-built soprano at Glyndebourne.

'I can't shift her,' he told the producer in rehearsal.

'Never mind, leave it to me,' the producer said.

And walking down the centre aisle of the stalls, he called out: 'Taxi! Taxi!'

Cyril Fletcher

BROADCASTER

I find opera so terribly funny that I have to keep away!

There is a true story of a distinguished vocal couple, however, Anne Ziegler and Webster Booth, I believe, who were singing the 'Trot Here and There' duet from Messager's *Veronique*.

She was on the swing. As she got on to it, she trapped his hand under her bottom. He could not withdraw it and had to trot here and there as she swung vigorously to and fro as they sang....

Gerald Moore

ACCOMPANIST

Peter Dawson, the Australian baritone and perhaps the most popular ballad singer in the 1920s told me that the Saturday night ballad concerts at Central Hall, Westminster, were so informal that there were no printed programmes; singers announced their items from the stage. I feel that the words, 'Saturday night' suggested a free and easy approach – at least to one singer, a tenor.

He had that 'week-end feeling'; he was very much the worse for wear and was more than a little unsteady on his feet. His opening offering was to be an aria from *La Reine de Saba*, a Gounod opera.

Now, the walk to the stage centre is a goodly stretch at Central Hall and Peter Dawson told me that before setting out on his trek to the piano, he saw the tenor eye his goal with a fixed stare as if threatening the instrument not to move. Then he set out bravely with his feet set at an angle of ten minutes to two, his arms bent at the elbow like stabilizers to keep his balance. Arriving miraculously at the piano – he was very short – he stood in its curve facing the audience with arms outstretched to left and right clutching the sturdy instrument as the blind Samson embraced the pillars in the halls of the Philistines. He waited. Then, taking a deep breath, he forsook the buttress which Steinway's had provided for him and took one step forward to announce his item.

In high pitched and choking tones he cried, 'Lend me your aid' – and fell flat on his face.

Whenever Victoria de los Angeles sings, her husband, Enrique Magrina, waits in the wings with a glass of water for Victoria to sip between groups at a recital.

At the Opera – Covent Garden, La Scala, Teatro Colon, the Met –

there he waits, ready and willing.

It was at the Metropolitan, New York, during a performance that Enrique really distinguished himself. Whether the opera was *La Bohème* or *Madam Butterfly* it hardly matters now, but Enrique had seen Victoria off – or rather on – at the prompt side, and knew that fifteen minutes later she would make her exit on the OP Side, and thither accordingly he would wend his way, carefully holding the precious glass of water. He knows backstage at the Met as well as any loving husband, but even so, you have to tread very lightly and watch very carefully where you are placing your feet on account of a spaghetti-like tangle of electric cable for stage lighting. What with the concentration on slow motion, on making no sound, on balance and avoidance, progress was made in low gear. Enrique had accomplished half his expedition when he heard a mighty 'whoosh' sound. Without moving his feet (those damned cables and the precious tumbler of water) he turned his head and there was the entire audience – diamond horseshoe and all – and every eye was on Mrs Magrina's little boy. He was discovered!

The cast almost stopped singing at the wonder of it all – and Victoria's lovely eyes almost popped out of her head. But, in the meantime, the storm centre of it stood there motionless, frozen stiff. In his own words:

'What do I do? Do I go backwards or forwards? I say "courage" to myself and I glide – bent almost double in an effort to make myself invisible – "onwards, forwards".'

That was not quite the end of the affair for there was a tiny cadenza. Within two minutes Sir Rudolph Bing, the General Manager, came backstage in a fury and demanded of Enrique:

'Who was that damned stage-hand walking across the stage with a glass of water?'

I take off my hat to Enrique for his reply was masterly; holding the glass behind him (now empty but still clasped in a hot hand) he said, after a fractional hesitation, 'I don't know.'

On this high note the only operatic appearance Enrique ever made was brought to a sudden and unapplauded close.

Conductors at rehearsal do not like it when some member of the orchestra (other than the leader) pops up to ask a question. Otto Klemperer was no exception.

'Herr Doktor,' called out a flautist on one occasion, 'do you want a *subito forte* at letter D?'

'Play what is written,' snapped Klemperer.

Ten minutes later, the same player stood up again:

'Herr Doktor, at the change of key two bars—'

'Play what is written,' interrupted the conductor.

After a lapse the irrepressible flautist popped up again:

'Maestro—' he started.

'By this time,' snarled Klemperer, 'call me Otto.'

From *Farewell Recital* by Gerald Moore (Hamish Hamilton, 1978).

Ruth Hall

JOURNALIST AND MUSICIAN

Cross-cultural confusion is common enough. Call it Eurogala in honour of the first elections to the European Parliament, put it on at a West End theatre and you have something different: an evening of such refined chaos as to attain the stature of art.

Last Sunday, the audience (black tie) were not quite sure how to deal with Lord Grade's mixture of pop, ballet, circus and classical music. They applauded every movement of the Vivaldi, hoping it was the last, and even managed to cheer half-way through the coda of Brahms's Academic Festival Overture. The performers came off little better. Two stars from La Scala, Milan, used to the operatic draw curtain, were completely thrown by the drop curtain at the Theatre Royal, which guillotined behind them as they took their bow. Refusing to go round the wings (blocked by television cables) they ended up pounding on the curtain with their fists unable to leave the stage.

Connoisseurs of the absurd cherished most, however, the evening's finale – a performance by the LSO Chorus and the hundred-strong EEC Youth Orchestra, expensively assembled for the occasion, of the last movement of Beethoven's 9th, whose theme, the 'Ode to Joy', is the EEC signature tune. Someone had decided they should play only the last six minutes of the movement which contains no recognizable statement of the 'Ode to Joy' theme. Confusion was worse confounded by the fact that microphones had been placed, pop-style, in front of the four soloists, whose tortured quartet drowned out both orchestra and choir. The resultant cacophony was such that the late Lord Mountbatten, nodding off in the Royal Box woke up and for some reason leapt to his feet. Exchanging quizzical looks his companions, Ted Heath and Roy Jenkins, followed suit, imitated by a puzzled audience.

There is a precedent. George II, asleep at the first performance of *The Messiah*, absentmindedly stood up during the Hallelujah chorus, thinking it was the national anthem. This quirk became a custom, now followed religiously. Maybe, after Mountbatten's initiative, the same will happen with Beethoven's 9th: at least we shall have that to our EEC credit.

[BD: With his highly developed sense of fun, Lord Louis, one imagines, would have been delighted to know of the effect produced by his 'dropping off'.]

From an article in the New Statesman, 25 May 1979.

Opera Interval

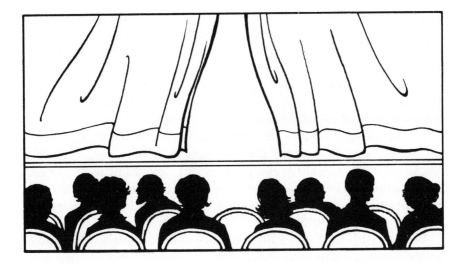

Joyce Grenfell

ACTRESS

Bravo – bravo. [Applauds] Oh how lovely. Wasn't it heavenly? Bravo – bravo!

Isn't she marvellous. That voice. It really is celestial. And he was *so* good, wasn't he? The one in the middle. The one in blue. You know, the main man. *Lovely* voice. [Gets up to let people pass] Can you manage?

Well now, shall we go out and *mingle* a little and see who is here – or shall we stay here and digest what we've just heard? Alright – digest now and mingle later.

D'you know I think that when I was *very very* young I heard Belushkin sing that apart, only he sang it lower. Yes, darling, I know the man tonight wasn't a bass but Belushkin was. He had this marvellous very low voice, I mean that's what he was famous for. I'm pretty sure it was him I heard in the part. I expect he sang it in a different key, that's all.

I must confess, I got a little confused in the story. Did you? I know she's a twin and there was a muddle, but I can't *quite* remember why she starts off in that pretty white dress and then when she comes in again later she's dressed as a crusader.

Yes. It probably *is* a disguise. But one wonders why? *She*'s the daughter of the man in black, I suppose. The one who sang at the top of the stairs with that lovely voice. Let's look it up and see who is who. 'Don Penzalo, a wealthy landowner' – that's probably her father. 'Mildura' – that's her, I think – 'daughter to the Duke of Pantilla'. Oh, not Don Penzalo then. No – 'the Duke of Pantilla, father of Mildura'. Well, there we are. I didn't think he was big enough.

'Zelda, an old nurse' – yes, we have seen her. She's the one with the rumbly voice, remember? Very bent, with two sticks. 'Fedora, a confidante, Boldoni, a bodyguard. Don Alfredo, a general in the crusaders.' Ah, crusaders! 'Chorus of fisherfolk, villagers, haymakers, courtiers and crusaders' – we haven't seen the courtiers and crusaders yet but we've seen the fisherfolk, villagers and haymakers – yes we have. They were the ones with the fishing-nets and rakes and things.

You know, one *ought* to do one's homework before one goes to the opera. I've got a little book that tells you all the stories but I can never remember to look it up before I get home and then it's too late.

Let's see what we have just seen: 'Act I: The Market Place of Pola. As dawn breaks over the sleepy village of Pola in Pantilla, fisherfolk on their way to work join with villagers and haymakers to express their concern over the royalist cause.' Oh – *that*'s what they were doing. 'Mildura pines for her lover, Don Alfredo, who is preparing to leave for the crusades' – ah, there you are – 'and disguises herself in order to join him in Malta.' Oh, Malta. Dear Malta. How I love it. Do you know Malta?

I used to go there a grade-eel when I was a gel, and one had such fun. I used to go and stay with darling old Admiral Sir Cardington Dexter and his wife Nadia. She was a *little* unusual! He met her in Casablanca! But I won't hear a word against her because she was always so kind to me. Oh it was such fun in those days. So gay. Parties, parties, and more parties. Heavenly young men in uniform – white *naval* uniform which is quite irresistible, and you know, honestly, one hardly noticed the Maltese at all.

Now. 'Mildura disguises herself in order to join Don Alfredo but Don Penzalo' – I'm sure he's the one in blue – 'seeks revenge for a slight done to him by the Duke and plans to abduct Mildura, whom he suspects of political duplicity, and flee with her to Spain.' Oh *Spain*. Very *mouvementé*!

Do you know Spain well? No, Italy is my passion. *Bella Italia*. I always feel very hard done by if I don't get my annual ration of *bella Italia*. It's so nourishing.

'Zelda, an old nurse, reads warnings in the stars and begs Mildura to delay her departure until the harvest is gathered in. Don Penzalo does not recognize Mildura and challenges her to a duet.' That's what it says: 'Challenges her to a du—.' Oh, I am idiotic. The

light's so bad in here. Oh, dear. They're back again. [*Gets up to let the people pass back to their seats*] I'm so sorry. Can you get by? Ow – no – it's all right, only a tiny little ladder. One really ought to come to the opera more often. I do love it so. My mother used to go a grade-eel. She loved it and of course she was very musical. Oh very. She had a most enchanting gift. She played the piano entirely by ear. She never had a lesson in her life. *Never.* She could go to an opera; hear it; and come home and play the *entire* thing from memory without a note of music. All the lovely tunes one knows so well. So you see, I was very lucky because I was brought up knowing all the lovely tunes one knows so well. It's such an advantage – one waits for them to happen and they *do*.

No, alas, I don't play. [*Sighs*] Now let's see what the next act holds in store for us.

'Act II: The cloisters of San Geminiano Cathedral.' I wonder if I've been there. So many lovely cathedrals all over *bella Italia*. 'Mildura, no longer disguised' – oh good – 'is on her way to Mass with her confidante Fedora, and Boldoni, a faithful bodyguard. Playfully she take off her chaplet of roses and puts it on Boldoni, who laughs.' That sounds rather fun. 'Don Alfredo, forewarned of Penzalo's plot, arrives unannounced at the cathedral with a band of crusaders, ostensibly to celebrate the feast of Saint Ogiano.'

Are you starving? Would you like an ice cream? Are you sure? It's a very long opera, three more acts. I should have fed you better. An egg isn't enough for opera. I do hope you don't wilt. No? I *love* it. I'm afraid it's all very nourishing for me. Oh the lights are going down. It's too exciting. I'm like a child in the theatre. [*Applauds*] I don't know who the conductor is but I believe he's very well known – Oh dear, we don't know where we are, do we? Yes we do. We're in the cloisters of the cathedral of San Geminiano. [*Turns round to hush other talkers*] Sh. Sh. Sh.

'Opera Interval' copyright © Joyce Grenfell.

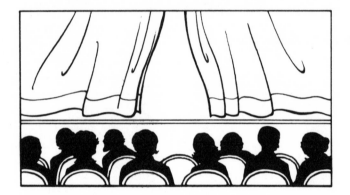

Derek Hammond-Stroud

BARITONE, ENGLISH NATIONAL OPERA

I had one of the most frightening moments in opera very early on in my career, during the first night of *Idomeneo* at the St Pancras Festival.

I was singing both Arbace and the Voice of Neptune, Neptune's having been recorded with trombones to be played back during the performance while I was on stage as Arbace.

At the crucial moment in the opera, when Idomeneo raises the sacrificial knife, Neptune should be heard forbidding Idomeneo to kill his son Idamante. But nothing happened. There was an empty silence. The play-back system had broken down.

Luckily I could remember the words of the aria and did the only thing possible. I turned my back on the audience and delivered Neptune's piece the best I could while the harpsichord filled in the harmonies.

The curtain fell at last at the end of what seemed to be a very long act to the relief of us all. Disaster had been averted: we could easily have come to a full stop.

On another occasion we very nearly didn't start at all. I was playing the role of Tonio in the English National Opera's production of *I Pagliacci* at the London Coliseum – a production so designed that it was necessary for me to come from one of the stage boxes in order to sing the prologue which starts the opera.

One cold winter night I was waiting outside the box ready to go on, the orchestral introduction having started, when I opened the door slightly, to check that all was in order. To my amazement someone inside firmly exclaimed, 'Go away! I'm in a draught' and promptly slammed the door in my face.

In a great panic and with much pulling and struggling with the door, I eventually convinced him that I had to sing the prologue and that the box was my stage entrance.

He capitulated finally and I arrived on stage just in time to sing 'A word allow me, ladies and gentlemen' – breathless but thankful that the box had no lock on the inside otherwise the opera would never have begun at all.

This didn't seem in the least funny at the time!

Vickers v. Zeffirelli

Jon Vickers raised American hackles by accusing Franco Zeffirelli of designing *Otello* for the Met in a way which caused immense 'confusions and problems' for the singers.

'I sing the first entrance from the poop of a ship that docks backwards. I am in a suit of armour which does not allow me to touch any part of my face with any part of my hands. In the dark I have to fight my way through ropes and cables, stand on a little box fourteen inches wide to sing, then climb a flight of stairs where every stair is of a different height. One is seven inches, another four and a half, another nine. Either I have to commit every step to memory or lower my head to watch my feet. In the last act Desdemona's bed is higher than my head. Putting Desdemona on the bed and strangling her is a gymnastic accomplishment, I can assure you.

'Zeffirelli's set is in keeping with his general low opinion of tenors.

'Zeffirelli is a genius. He knows what he does. Everything is intentional . . . I shall never do another new production with him.'

From an article in the *Evening Standard*, 8 February 1978.

Hinge and Bracket

POPULAR LADY DUETTISTS

A reporter was fortunate enough recently to find Dame Hilda Bracket and Doctor Evadne Hinge at their lovely house in Stackton Tressel, deep in the heart of the Suffolk countryside, where the ladies were enjoying a brief sabbatical between their extensive touring commitments – 'so important to have somewhere to relax', as Dame Hilda says. As many readers will know, the ladies are still very active in the world of music in general and opera in particular.

HILDA ... poor Jean Batkin – a very serviceable contralto – big gel, y'know – but I suppose it was her own fault – the incident with the Mars Bars was the last straw....

REPORTER I beg your pardon?

EVADNE Dame Hilda is, of course, referring to something which took place many years ago while we were touring with the Rosa Charles Opera Company. And may I say how pleased we are to have the opportunity to mention in print some of the wonderful British opera singers who were active in the period just after the war. People like Milford Pleight—

HILDA Ah, yes. That is 'Plate', as in crockery. Charming man, the voice of Caruso, the looks of Arnold Pilbeam. He was, I recall, an astonishing Ramades – *Tosca*, of course.

EVADNE *Aida*, dear.

HILDA Quite! Do you know, from the very first day of rehearsal he had his part firmly under control – amazing man. And then, of course, there were many other men in the Rosa Charles who could easily have had an international career. One thinks of Bradford Tweats ...

EVADNE ... who played a wonderful Sarastro to Dame Hilda's

Pamina.

HILDA Indeed. Do you know, every performance he would spend a good ten minutes encouraging me just before my entrance. Such consideration is rare today.

EVADNE Yes. That season of *The Magic Flute* was most successful. It would have been even more so but for the very inadequate soprano who was singing the Queen of the Night. What was her name again, dear – ?

HILDA Sibylla Strang. Not one of our strongest singers – voice like a pin. Of course, she never liked you, dear.

EVADNE What do you mean?

HILDA Well, it was that habit of yours of referring to her as Stringy Sibyl!

EVADNE Oh, yes. Of course. I'd forgotten that – Stringy Sibyl! [*Convulsions of stringy Doctor Hinge*]

HILDA Well, one had to admit, in general the women in the company were weaker than the men. In particular the sopranos had been badly trained. Remember Flavia Chequettes –

EVADNE Oh yes. Big voice. No control.

HILDA Quite a *promising* voice, unfortunately ruined by bad teaching. Now, of course, my *own* teacher had all the right ideas. In at the deep end. Do you know, he had me in *A Masked Ball* when I was sixteen? I don't think even Dame Eva Turner could say that.

EVADNE Oh, she can. It's just that she prefers saying *Un Ballo in Maschera* much more.

HILDA And, of course, he gave me *Götterdämmerung* when I was barely eighteen. But, you see, when I first joined the Rosa Charles, they didn't have anyone of my abilities and consequently I was handling enormous parts while I was still virtually a gel. They seemed to think I had the vocal wherewithal to deal with six or seven different ones in a week!

EVADNE Of course, one of the reasons for that was that your understudy was so frequently indisposed.

HILDA Oh yes. Poor gel: Dodie Bantock. She had quite a pleasant voice but unfortunately was always having trouble with her throat. I can still see her in the final throes of *Traviata* with a woollen scarf round her throat over a crêpe bandage. Of course it fitted in with the part in that particular case, but it did look rather incongruous in *Salome*. She married the company accountant,

Courtneigh Pines, a very *dull* man – and after they left for the honeymoon nobody ever saw them again. There was a rumour that they had formed a double act, Bantock and Pines – he was a reasonable amateur bassoonist – which after six months or so lapsed into well-merited oblivion. And then, of course, there was Nunton Odstock—

EVADNE Dear Nunton—

HILDA Big chap . . . six foot two or three, and a wonderful dancer – very light on my feet. He was very involved with the leading cellist in our orchestra – what was that gel's name again, dear?

EVADNE *His* name was Burton Coggles. And I don't think involved is quite the right word.

HILDA Well. They used to share digs, you know, things like that—

EVADNE Of course, if we're mentioning singers of the past, we could never leave out Giulietta Cotodratta—

HILDA Spanish soprano – highly temperamental – she used to run round backstage before every performance beating her breast like King Kong and shouting at the top of her voice, 'I can't go on, I can't go on' – and then, she couldn't: no breath left.

REPORTER Fascinating, Dame Hilda, but I wonder if we could go back to the incident with the Mars Bars which you mentioned earlier. . . ?

HILDA Yes. Of course. It happened like this. Towards the end of our time with the Rosa Charles, Doctor Hinge had virtually taken control of the whole company, or at least the production side, and we decided to mount a special production of *Hansel and Gretel* for Christmas.

EVADNE That's right, and in the interest of realism, I had arranged for the gingerbread house in the last act to be decorated with real sweets. Dame Hilda and I spent the entire day cutting up Mars Bars and sticking them round the walls.

HILDA Of course, we had a magnificent cast – the mother was played by Phoebe Lateral, and the father was Bradford Tweats – such a pleasure to work with him again. I myself played Hansel – they all said I had the legs for it, and I didn't mind showing them. My Gretel was Pinky Willets. If I remember, Topsey Hodgetts handled the Sandman and the Dew Fairy. But the problem was Jean Batkin who was singing the Witch.

EVADNE We did not know, you see, that she had an inordinately sweet tooth ... and a passion for Mars Bars.

HILDA All during the first act, in which she did not appear, she had steadily chewed her way through Evadne's painstaking embellishments to the gingerbread house—

EVADNE —egged on by Bradford Tweats who had a peculiar sense of humour.

HILDA And so, of course, the curtain rose on the Witch's house only to find that Evadne's gastronomic marvel had turned to a dismal shack.

EVADNE Well, naturally, poor Jean had to go. We would normally have substituted Roma Wartski, a contralto who often guested with us, but unfortunately she was not available.

HILDA Fortunately, we were able to fall back on Gladys Etheridge, one of our own stalwarts – she was to us what Edith Coates was to Sadler's Wells.

REPORTER Well. It's been fascinating talking to you two ladies—

HILDA Just a moment, dear. I haven't finished yet. I was going to tell you about Vesta Bewles, the well-known vocal coach. In fact, curiously enough, I had a letter just the other day from someone who claimed to remember me singing with the Carl Rosa in 1938 – well, of course, I had to reply pointing out that she was obviously confusing me with. . . .

The human cannon ball

At a performance of *Hansel and Gretel* with the Carl Rosa Opera Company in Liverpool an over-anxious Dew Fairy stood fretting in the trapdoor machinery under the stage, convinced that she had missed her entrance. Finally snapping under the strain, she rounded on a passing stage-hand and in a voice which made it clear that she would stand for no nonsense, demanded the trap be fired forthwith.

The man obliged – and the audience was amazed to see the lady shoot up through the floor so rapidly she fell in an unoperatic heap on the boards.

Since her first line as she struggled to her feet was something about 'being up in the morning early', the audience collapsed and the Dew Fairy fled.

[BD: By chance, I recently found out who the Dew Fairy was. As a gentleman . . .]

It must be true:
my wife read it in the paper

I never thought I would see the day when an opera producer would go so far as to present a gothic cathedral, mediaeval houses and a midsummer meadow in, of all works, *Die Meistersinger*. David Poutney, who is full of revolutionary ideas, claims he found it all in the libretto. 'There is scarcely one stage direction I have not followed,' he said.

It is true, of course. It *is* all there.   *The Guardian*

I am a regular visitor to the Coliseum, and I have a request. Please could someone get a tall ladder and clean those lions and cupids. If it needs a pair of hands and a long brush, I'll volunteer.

Letter to the *Evening News*

The audience at the Coliseum found themselves involved in an industrial dispute one evening that – remarkably – involved no striking. A note handed out with the programme for one perform-ance of the ENO's *Il Trovatore* regretted that 'owing to contractual problems with Equity the Chorus in Act II will be without anvils'.

Daily Telegraph

It is stated that Herr Wagner has left Britain not one penny the richer. The receipts at the Albert Hall were, it appears, not suffi-cient to pay both him and the vocalists.

Birmingham Daily Post, June 1877

In the British Honours List the arts are represented by film actor Laurence Olivier who receives a knighthood for his services to the stage and the same award for services to music went to Dr Alcom, a sergeant.   *Daily Gleaner* (Jamaica)

Rhydderch Davies, for eighteen years a principal singer at Covent Garden, sought High Court damages for injuries received during a first night performance of *Billy Budd*. Mr Davies alleges that during the performance, while another singer was singing 'Look where you go', he fell into a sunken lighting pit, fracturing a foot and a shoulder. *Evening Standard*

Stage Show, The Marsham Singers: Next year's main stage show is to be a 'serious' operatic work, though what it will be is still to be decided.

Serious works already performed are *The Bartered Bridge* and *Don Glovani*. The chosen work, will, of course, have to reflect a realistic view of the society's musical resources.

Government Department Newsletter

The opera held in the Good Templar's Hall was a great success. Special thanks, though, are due to the vicar's daughter who laboured the whole evening at the piano, which as usual fell upon her. *South African newspaper*

Caballé and the Spanish mode

Monserrat Caballé recently gave a recital at La Scala accompanied only by her pianist Miguel Zanetti, opening with some liturgical arias from Vivaldi, followed by romantic songs from Pergolesi, Marcello and Palsiello, finally closing with some Spanish songs by Granados and Obrados.

The audience demanded more and Caballé generously sang an encore and then another and then another. (Caballé is a generously-endowed lady, after all.) By the time she reached encore number seven, also a Spanish song, she was unable to resist adding a little footwork. She may even have longed for a pair of castanets, so strong was the Spanish mode upon her. In the event she put in a few graceful flamenco steps – and then slipped, albeit gracefully, and found herself subsided on the floor.

Having fallen, she did not rise, nor did Zanetti stop playing. She carried on with her fiery fandango, propped up on one elbow.

Her fans were ecstatic and crowded down to the footlights to applaud her as she was helped up.

Harry Secombe

COMEDIAN AND SINGER

During the run of *The Four Musketeers* at the Theatre Royal, Drury Lane, in which I played d'Artagnan, the matinées in the summer months tended to be fairly sparsely attended. Sometimes, when it was particularly hot, the exit doors to the stalls were left open.

Occasionally this resulted in unexpected non-paying customers slipping into the empty seats. They were not regular theatre-goers. Indeed, they paid no attention to what was going on on-stage at all. Instead they were deeply engrossed in putting away as much methylated spirits as they could drink. Inevitably this resulted in raucous disagreement and downright bad temper.

Now, it is difficult enough to keep the audience from flagging at the best of times on a hot and sticky afternoon but on this occasion the noise from the non-payers was too much – even for me.

We were in the middle of a big scene involving the whole cast, two sopranos, a horse and myself going flat out while down in the front stalls a counter-plot broke out.

Enough is enough, I thought.

I stepped forward, sword in hand and held it up to the conductor. He stopped the orchestra. I addressed the rowdies.

'Do you mind keeping quiet,' I screamed reasonably, 'some of us are trying to get some sleep up here.'

John Vickers as Tristan

Fifty-five minutes of *Tristan and Isolde* were lost at Covent Garden when Vickers abruptly truncated his performance by retiring for the final act.

After the second interval Colin Davis strode on to the stage and announced to cries of 'money back!' that only twenty minutes of Act III could be performed without Vickers, who was incapacitated by hay fever.

Vickers had been attempting to restore himself with hay fever treatments but he was afraid of losing his voice altogether. He had not actually sneezed on-stage but someone in the audience described him as 'wheezing through'.

After retreating to his dressing-room Vickers decided not to emerge even for the final minutes of Act III when Tristan is on-stage, all but dead and therefore mute. As a result an actor who had played a small part in Act I put on Vickers' costume and played the dying Tristan, omitting his one cry of 'Isolde' as he dies.

'He played the part very well,' an official of the company said, 'considering Isolde has to prostrate herself on top of him. He just lay on his stomach and didn't move.'

From Londoner's Diary, *Evening Standard*, 8 June 1978.

David Gillard

CRITIC

It was a performance of *Don Giovanni* at Covent Garden in June 1976; in my review I called it 'the night the Don took a step towards hell an act early'.

John Copley was using a built-up false stage to give added rake to the production and, in the closing stages of Act I, a section of the false stage gave way suddenly, plunging the Don (the Italian baritone Ruggiero Raimondi) down to his knees like a pantomime devil going down a trap.

It was quite obvious that Raimondi didn't think it in the least funny and he stumbled about in his little trench looking very angry until Sir Geraint Evans (Leporello) helped pull him clear, limping and with a bent sword.

There was a great deal of banging and crashing during the interval as the stage was hammered together again. As far as I know, it never collapsed again and also as far as I know, Raimondi never returned after that season of performances.

I also recall a performance of *Carmen*. In Act I of Michael Geliot's production, a little local colour had been added to the town square scene by adding a donkey to mingle with the townsfolk and soldiers.

The animal was supposed to hold back from walking through an archway with a load on his back and some members of the chorus had been deputed to shove it from behind to get it moving.

All very well save that this donkey was particularly mulish and didn't want to hold back. Those of us sitting near the stage were treated to the sight of a hand, holding a length of knotted rope appearing from the archway. The rope was waved in front of the animal's face in an effort to keep it back – all this while the chorus still shoved from behind to get it to go on. The beast can hardly have known whether it was coming or going. Eventually hand and dangling rope disappeared and the donkey trotted in, no doubt to his relief and certainly to all others concerned!

Elektra shocks

The East German producer, Harry Kupfer, thought hopefully that he had managed to overcome the difficulties which his production of Strauss's Elektra had met with on its opening in Amsterdam.

The point at issue was that his critics complained that the Fifth Maid, who disappears near the beginning of the opera, came on again later stark naked to be killed off as a ritual sacrifice – a piece of business which had not actually occurred to the composer.

Kupfer restaged the work for the Welsh National Opera and made it clear that the slain girl is a slave and not the Fifth Maid. Moreover, he insisted, the confusion at Amsterdam was caused by the fact that both parts were played by black girls whose faces the critics had not recognized.

In Cardiff, Kupfer cast the maid as white and the slave as black in order to put a stop to any further argument – or so he hoped.

As it happened, the critics still complained that the libretto does not call for a nude sacrifice.

[BD: But at least they knew which girl they were arguing about.]

Charles Oxtoby

SOUTH AFRICAN BROADCASTING CORPORATION

I have been collecting operatic horror stories for some years and have come to the conclusion that a lot of the trouble is caused by what I call 'the engineering'. Even in the eighteenth century critics were remarking on the ridiculous effects produced when some careless stage manager missed his cue and forgot to fly in on time – the result in one opera was that the curtain went up on the lead tenor in full-bottomed wig, elegantly taking snuff seated at the bottom of the ocean.

Down the years this sort of thing has added colour to more or less straight performances.

In *The Flying Dutchman* at Covent Garden in 1899, the ship never made the quay in Act I: the audience was treated instead to a terrible series of grunts and groans until a clear voice, loud enough to top the orchestra, bawled:

'Why don't yer *shove* 'er along, Bill!'

'Ow the 'ell, can I?' came an exasperated reply, '– the perisher's stuck.'

Not even Wagner's beloved festival theatre at Bayreuth was immune. During *Parsifal* with a Belgian tenor, Ernest van Dyck, in the title role, he stepped too far up-stage [BD: a familiar manoeuvre] and his flowing golden wig caught on a branch of the mystic forest at the moment of the transformation. Vines, leaves, trees, began to rise – with them, van Dyck's wig. As it lifted, revealing an inevitably bald head, the distraught tenor leapt into the air, grabbed it – and promptly dropped it on to the floor.

He stooped to pick it up, realized he was supposed to be singing, and so rammed it back on to his head, going into his aria.

He put it on back to front in his haste and all the audience could see was the end of his nose.

Not all mishaps are unpremeditated. Chaliapin was roundly detested by the backstage crew at the New York Met because of his high and mighty manner – and once they were able to do something about it during a performance of Massenet's *Don Quixote*. The stage-hands who had to hoist him on to his mule in the wings managed to stick a pin into the animal at the same time so that Chaliapin shot on to the stage on a bucking, kicking fury. He had his work cut out to hold on, let alone sing.

There was an unusual disaster in 1850 in a production of Auber's *Fra Diavolo* in Brussels. The part of the Englishman was being played for the first time by a singer from the Paris Opera. There is a scene where Milord is informed by a small captain of the local *gendarmerie* that brigands are in the immediate neighbourhood. The scene is on the first floor of an hotel. A window at the back of the stage is open and through it can be seen the spire of the village church. Milord (fortunately intentionally comic) is in dressing-gown and slippers and when told the news, reels back in terror.

According to the stage directions he is supposed to *nearly* fall out of the window, saving himself at the last moment only by spreading his arms wide. In this case the window of the Brussels stage was wider than the one in Paris to which the singer was accustomed, with the result that his hands never touched the window frames at all. He went straight through. All the audience could see were his red slippers poking up against the top of the church steeple. The little captain hauled him back in, which convulsed the house and stopped the orchestra. Every now and then throughout the rest of the evening the incident would come to mind and titters would arise here and there in the auditorium affecting singers and musicians as well.

Audiences in the seventeenth and eighteenth centuries had a passion for lavish spectacle. In a letter to Alexander Pope, Lady Mary Wortley Montague described a visit to a performance in Vienna in 1716:

The stage was built over a very large canal on which, at the beginning of

the second act, there came from different parts fleets of gilded vessels that gave a representation of a naval battle.

What Lady Mary did not know was that the setting had set the emperor back something like £50,000 in today's money.

Wagner influenced stage machinery a great deal and made considerable demands on his technicians. When *Das Rheingold* was first produced he insisted that the Rhine Maidens were to swim even though he had no way of introducing water on to the stage. The problem was solved by having each Maiden attached to something like a portable music-stand mounted on a small truck and trundled about the stage by the stage crew concealed by strategically placed rocks. What the Maidens thought about it no one seems to have recorded.

Transformation scenes were another problem, as was Wagner's determination that Alberich should become alternatively visible and invisible by means of the Tarnhelm. To bring this about Wagner invented a steam curtain. The steam was released from rows of jets along the line of the footlights which gave it whatever colour was needed – usually pink – and a black curtain lowered a short distance behind the jets. This device was used (apparently without anyone being scalded) to hide Alberich and also change scenes.

To keep his stage crew on their toes further, Wagner also introduced animals, the most famous of which is, of course, Grane. At Covent Garden he used to be played by a decrepit old cab horse who always grazed on the scenery, possibly to take his mind off the fire which he hated. The English National Opera have solved the problem by having Grane as a film-projection.

Sometimes it is the producer who is responsible for killing his own work stone dead. Verdi's now forgotten opera *I Masnadiere* is an example. In one scene, the Duke laments that through the ingratitude of his sons he has been reduced to a starved and emaciated wretch.

At the first performance at Her Majesty's, London, in 1847, Lablache, a famous bass, was chosen for the part. He was then fifty-three, an ample, well-nourished figure. The sight of his lamenting his lean and hungry look was too much for the audience and hoots of laughter greeted every line which was supposed to bring tears to their eyes. Lablache was furious and suspected Verdi of having had a joke played on him. He never sang the part again.

Lablache had a voice to fit his physique and sang often with Antonio Tamburini, another powerful singer. Rossini, after hearing them sing together in Paris, wrote to a friend in Italy: 'Lablache and Tamburini sang the duet from Bellini's *I Puritani*. I need not tell you anything about their performance. You surely heard it for yourself.'

Sometimes a librettist, because of social convention, would have to leave more to the imagination than he would nowadays.

A typical example is *Fra Diavalo* which caused a mini-uproar in Heidelberg. The work is rarely performed, which is not surprising since it is not up to much, but word went round the university that it was the first opera to feature a strip-tease.

In Act II, Zerlina, the heroine, is in her bedroom on the eve of her wedding. Unknown to her, so are Fra Diavolo and two of his friends. As Zerlina expresses in a somewhat florid aria her joy at the delights tomorrow will bring, she starts to get ready for bed.

The audience was treated to an unforgettable spectacle.

While the three ruffians on the stage, peered, guffawed and sniggered behind their screen, the portly Zerlina peeled off. One by one, shapeless bits of chiffon, cotton, silk, and wool were unhooked, unpinned, unbuttoned and untied. The situation grew more and more ludicrous as each unveiling left the monumental beauty as well-concealed as before.

There came the moment when someone's nerve went in the audience and he started to giggle. Grins changed to titters, titters to general giggling, giggling to laughter and when at last the mountain of maidenliness, as fully-clothed as ever, hoisted herself into bed, the theatre was filled with an unstoppable blaze of laughter. The expression on Zerlina's face showed the humour of the situation had not passed her by either.

Mishaps involving prime donne seem to have been less common than you might expect given that until recently they were, almost by definition, a bit on the big side. Tosca's leap has been mentioned earlier in this book, but here's a variation: one Tosca refused to jump at all! She astonished the audience by majestically disappearing from view by walking down a flight of steps she'd had put up behind the scenery.

Genuine misfortune struck the German soprano Theresa Tietjens who flourished in the last half of the last century. She was singing the title role in *Norma* and at a solemn moment had to strike a huge gong with an appropriately substantial drumstick. At one performance, Tietjens swung back the stick with great flourish – and caught the tenor, standing directly behind her, a demolishing thwack on the nose which put him out for some time, totally wrecking the scene, if not the opera.

Conductors seem to carry very little responsibility for disaster.

There was once a *Punch* cartoon which showed a performance about to begin. On-stage the singers are dressed in traditional Wagnerian gear – white-robed ladies, armed men with spears, helmets, hunting-horns and so forth.

Through the slowly-opening curtain can be seen the conductor with upraised arms, surrounded by his players.

One of the singers, her hand clamped over her mouth in horror, is saying to the one standing next to her:

'Oh, my God! He's played the overture to Carmen!'

Upstaging on four legs

It was W. C. Fields, of course, who warned all actors who wanted their reputations to remain intact always to refuse to appear in a play or a film with children or animals. Glyndebourne had this brought home to them in a touring production of *L'Elisir d'Amour* in which a donkey stole the headlines in most of the places they

visited, not only during the performances but in advance as well.

Had the company been able to tour its own donkey things might have been different – but they couldn't. The donkeys engaged were local animals and in consequence irresistible to local news editors when being 'auditioned'. At Liverpool, there were three contenders for the part, Ringo, Toby and Jenny. Ringo did best at his audition and went on to play Manchester where he got even more publicity.

The northern edition of one of the national dailies went so far as to devote its notice almost entirely to Ringo, his temperament, the part he played, his owners and his diet. To be fair, there was a brief, but reassuring, postscript which read: 'The opera itself is superbly presented.'

For George V's Silver Jubilee, Covent Garden mounted a special production of *Prince Igor*. At the first performance, at the end of the prologue when the Prince leads off his army to glorious war, two horses were brought on, one for Igor, the other for his son. Charles Kullman (the son) mounted without difficulty but Herbert Janssen (Igor) got stuck – head and arms dangling over one side, legs over the other. Beecham was conducting and not even his presence prevented the giggling which swept the house as Igor galloped off like a sack of potatoes.

Such unseemliness was prevented at further performances by the tactful introduction of four grooms, one at each corner of the horse to give Igor a leg-up.

Few cats seem interested in opera (or indeed are involved) but there are two stories from Sadler's Wells. One involves the cat who eased the tension in *Cavalleria Rusticana* by strolling nonchalantly across the stage flicking her tail at the orchestra. On another night, the theatre cat (who could often be seen sunning himself outside the Stage Door) found himself on-stage by some geographical error while Rigoletto lamented over Gilda in her sack.

After an initial bit of tittering, the audience managed to keep its attention on the opera.

The cat had a slightly different reaction. The moment he realized the audience was in he 'froze', then crept slowly down to the

footlights, belly close to the floor peering into the darkness of the auditorium. He was trying to make out what all those people were *doing*.

Covent Garden had a kitten who appeared in *Die Meistersinger*. In Act II with Hans Sachs banging away at his shoes and Beckmesser making a mess of his serenade, the kitten edged his way along the scenery behind Sachs, jumped down on to the floor and crept up close to Beckmesser's shoes and sat gazing up at him, tail pointing straight out. Suddenly Sachs slammed down his hammer and the kitten, taken by surprise, skittered sideways into the wings. A gust of laughter swept the house and the baritone, who hadn't noticed the cat at all, congratulated himself on how well his performance was going that evening.

Leo Slezac (Austrian tenor and Wagnerian, 1873–1946), well down-stage, was in full voice, when a large black cat lifted the backcloth and walked in a stately manner down to the footlights and sat down in front of him, facing the audience and began to wash its hands and face. Slezac, put out by the roaring hilarity of the audience, looked all round him – but couldn't see the cat until the conductor pointed his baton at the animal.

Still singing, Slezac picked up the cat, tucked him under one arm and carried him off to the wings, returning, dusting his hands, to thunderous applause.

While not actually on-stage, the handsome herd of Friesians at

Glyndebourne are musically aware as well as being pretty to look at. Hans Werner Henze has first-hand proof of this in a story he tells about the first night of the British première of his *Elegy for Young Lovers*.

During an interval, someone in the picknicking throng noticed that all the cattle had moved right away from the Opera House and were standing on the top of a hill nearby. 'What', someone asked George Christie, 'are your cattle doing up there?'

'Well, they'd much sooner be down here,' Christie replied, 'that is – when we're not performing Henze!'

There was once a Pyrenean mountain dog called Booboo who appeared with Sadler's Wells' *Carmen* in Bournemouth.

No one was more astonished than his owner, who was in the audience.

Booboo had last been seen the previous afternoon and had been officially reported to the police as missing. (No one was unduly worried – Pyrenean mountain dogs don't stay missing for long.)

According to the newspapers, Booboo decided to reappear in *Carmen* at a moment when only three principals were on-stage.

One of the chorus entered 'unobtrusively' (a difficult thing to do when the stage is only populated by three people and a dog) and tried to shoo Booboo away. Booboo wasn't having anything of that. He was enjoying himself too much. He ignored the conductor and strolled round the stage several times, grinning amiably at everyone, deftly getting out of the way every time anyone made a grab for him. Finally the action had to stop. He was caught by a flying tackle by Don José (Jon Andrew) who staggered manfully away with 130 lbs of dog in his arms. Carmen (Joyce Blackham) collapsed laughing.

After the curtain had come down on the end of the act, the cast gathered round making a great fuss of Booboo while his owner went back to collect him. 'I can't understand it,' he said. 'He's been here before, but he's never wanted to go on the stage as far as I know.'

Lohengrin's swan is world-famous for being missed, if you believe all the stories you hear. I don't, but there is an apparently definitive version involving Herr Slezac (again). Slezac was fond of a bottle of good wine in his dressing-room and, during a performance of *Lohengrin* in Berlin, stayed for an extra tipple and arrived late for his cue, just in time to see the swan set sail without him.

Slightly unsteady on his feet, without ceremony and interrupting the solo, he turned back into the wings and shouted: 'Hey! What time's the next swan?'

A. C. Benson as Lohengrin met with an unusual swan-uppance when he appeared standing in the boat at precisely the right moment, this time only to find that the swan slowed down until it finally stopped – and so did the music. The silence was broken only by the creaking sound of straining ropes as the stage crew fought to draw the swan further on-stage. They failed. There was a sharp cracking sound, caused by the swan's head and neck snapping off and flying into the wings.

Benson walked the rest of the way.

[BD: This correspondence is now closed.]

John Collins

HOUSE MANAGER, ROYAL OPERA HOUSE
1957–72

It is generally supposed that a House Manager has nothing much to do during the day till shortly before seven o'clock in the evening when he puts on his dress clothes and a bright smile to welcome in the audience for the performance. As it happened, I was usually at my desk by ten o'clock, managing the house.

To make my point: I remember one evening, about ten minutes after the curtain had gone up, I decided to inspect the buffet in the Crush Bar. A new waitress, passing me, enquired kindly: 'By the way, Mr Collins, what do you do during the day? Are you a bank manager?'

Technically, a House Manager's jurisdiction ends at the audience side of the orchestra pit – except for those ritualistic occasions which everyone dreads: the slight fumbling and parting of those imposing curtains to enable the wretched House Manager to step forward with the news that Miss X had been suddenly indisposed and her place will be taken instead by Miss Y.

The gods start to groan before you even open your mouth.

On one such occasion, I had a different sort of request to make, but one which filled me with equal apprehension: 'Is there a doctor in the house?'

The lead singer had fainted away into the arms of her lover (a piece of business not called for in the libretto). The curtain was down, the whole cast gathered in a circle and Solti had come up from the pit.

'Well, go on,' he hissed at me. 'Do something!'

I knew full well what I had to do. I was equally well aware that the film of *Doctor in the House* was doing good business in the West End.

I cleared my throat, fingered the curtains and stepped in front trying not to look too nervous to make my plea. I need have had no worry at all. There was not a single titter. All that happened was that six men rushed forward from the stalls and the problem was solved.

[BD: It has been suggested that half the stalls had in fact drifted out to the bar, believing the act to be finished, but can this not be put down to partisan rumour by supporters of another house not a hundred miles away?]

On-stage, I have been told that I look much like the conductor Bryan Balkwill. On an evening when I *did* have an announcement to make about a change of cast, I had no sooner stepped back through the curtain than Bryan entered the pit. Dame Eva Turner buttonholed me in the foyer in the first interval. 'How on earth,' she asked, 'did you manage to get down there so quickly?'

To return to the occasion of my being accused of being a bank manager manqué, one particular evening finished around one o'clock the following morning, having been a glittering but totally exhausting state gala. My wife and I, both in our evening clothes, left the Opera House to walk round to Floral Street where I had parked my car about fifteen hours earlier.

There we found two tough lorry-drivers from the market rocking the vehicle to and fro in order to move it. Feeling dead-beat, I said: 'I wish you wouldn't do that to my car.'

'It's orl right for you toffs,' came the reply. 'You've been enjoying yerselves all night. Some of us 'ave to work for a living, don't we?'

During my time at the Opera House I met a great many well-known people, sometimes in bizarre circumstances. There was, for instance, the night I encountered a film star I had adored for years.

The lady was storming round the foyer, furious because a doorman would not let her back into the auditorium, the curtain having gone up. The man telephoned me in my office to tell me what was going on and I decided I had better go down full of suitable apologies in order to restore calm. And, after all, this was the chance of a lifetime to meet *the* star. Carefully checking hair and tie, I walked quickly down the staircase smiling apologetically. But the moment she clapped eyes on me, she bawled:

'You the manager?! Right! How do I get out of this goddam place?'

She *didn't* say goddam. But she *was* Ava Gardner.

The Opera House's elegant Crush Bar is used from time to time for Government receptions. At one of these I was slightly surprised, there being so many distinguished guests in the party, to be drawn aside by an aide of the Foreign Secretary. Taking my arm, he said:

'I say, old chap, you must come and meet the Prime Minister of Bulgaria.'

'Well, I'd be delighted—' I had started to say, when the aide cut in with:

'I've just got to get the Foreign Secretary on his own for a few moments.'

Still, it's not everybody who has met the Prime Minister of Bulgaria. . . .

Lord Holderness

FORMER GOVERNMENT MINISTER

I was in the audience at the performance of *Rigoletto* when Anna Moffo suddenly and unexpectedly fainted away during a duet with Peter Glossop.

Knowing the opera less well then than I do now, I was less surprised than I should be now to see Glossop tighten his grip on Moffo and nobly sustain his part in their duet; but even with my then lack of knowledge, it was easy to recognize the look of profound relief when Glossop saw that the curtain was being brought down prematurely.

Alberto Remedios

INTERNATIONAL WAGNERIAN TENOR

As Siegfried on tour in Leeds, I had finished my first scene in Act I, strode off-stage expressing great joy at having found my father's sword, Nothung, and vowing to come back later to forge it. When I re-entered to do this, I found that the anvil on which I was supposed to operate and which I was supposed to split in half with one mighty blow, was already in two pieces.

My Mime (Paul Crook) had sat on it.

It wasn't his fault. Some of the bolts were missing.

I had to forge the sword on half an anvil and wave it above my head in triumph as the curtain came down on Act I.

In *Götterdämmerung* at the Coliseum the river scene with the Rhinemaidens is represented by strips of coloured ribbon which weave up and down in waves – rather like spaghetti.

One performance several of the motors which operate the strips 'blew' and stopped the waves altogether – which left me trying to see the conductor, audience and Rhinemaidens through a fog of smoke, the smell of burning oil and piles of inert spaghetti through which I had to fight to get from one side of the stage to the other.

Back to Siegfried, this time in San Diego, where the Wanderer, Noel Tyle, seemed to me to be nearly seven feet tall – which made me feel like a midget. He came striding past a rock on his entrance, banged his spear on it and severely weakened it at the joint where I am supposed to shatter it later in the scene. He had to hold it in place so it didn't fall off before I could get at it. He also had to mutter (while still singing):

'Don't hit it too hard – the goddam thing's broken already!'

Ralph Koltai

STAGE DESIGNER

We spent some time for the English National Opera's production of *The Ring* in trying to determine the best method for splitting the anvil when Siegfried strikes his blow. The idea of the stage management operating a remote control device from the wings was considered but finally dismissed because of the difficulty of ensuring precise synchronization.

We therefore decided on a foot-pedal mechanism attached to the up-stage side of the anvil to be operated by Alberto Remedios himself at the moment of impact. The pedal was painted white to be clearly visible to the singer. The system worked splendidly – until one evening when Alberto, with more than his customary abandon and exuberant virile excess in this scene, trod on the pedal while still filing away at the bits of the sword, some five minutes before the intended moment – with the obvious result.

Of course, Wagnerian audiences, being quite a breed apart from the rest of humanity, behaved with expected decorum. There was hardly a titter. After all, Reginald Goodall was still working away in the pit and Alberto kept his cool, filing away on half an anvil!

Millicent Martin

ENTERTAINER

Millicent Martin made her first appearance on the stage at the Royal Opera House in the children's chorus of *The Magic Flute*. It is not that particular opera which stands out in her mind, though. It is *Carmen*:

'I was doing the relieving guard and there was so much snow falling on London – a real blizzard – that only three of us turned up.

'After we had sung the children's chorus, we were given a huge round of applause, not only from the audience but by everyone on stage!

'We were *so* proud.'

Caryl Brahms

AUTHOR AND CRITIC

'But you must have seen so many mishaps in the theatre – all those unrehearsed effects,' the unknown voice on the telephone insisted ghoulishly.

Up flicked, as though I were drowning, or so they tell us, a series of scenes from my own disastrous past in theatres hardly able to hold up their marquées for the shame I brought upon them.

That night at Blackpool with *A Bullet in the Ballet* when a truck on which a scene was set up-stage had a faulty – or possibly Fawlty – anchor. The truck broke loose and so did all hell as it trundled down-stage stopping only just short before what Fokine, the great choreographer, called 'zee tootsies'. Two stars and two walk-on ladies and 'as cast' bit-part players made for the door at the side of the truck, inelegantly and in vain. It was not a practical door, just a daub of paint on a wall of canvas. Nothing for it but for them to scramble off to a raucous accompaniment of jeers from the auditorium, in all too evident disarray.

Same play: different city. In fact, Edinburgh. One of the stars – same star – had insisted on playing a scene with a *soi-disante* theatre cleaner in the actual auditorium. This little whimsy could end only in tears, we warned him. And so it did, for at that point in the pre-London run (wishful thinking that pre-London, for we closed for ever and by mutual consent after Liverpool) a new ASM joined us. Dutifully he locked the pass door and the stage waited while the star pounded round the entire block outside the theatre to arrive on-stage with a stitch which doubled him up.

Then there was the Royal Charity Gala at Drury Lane when, in the presence of my future monarch, something went wrong with the sound and though the all-black cast loyally continued to open and shut their mouths under their gigantic carnival hats, not a word could be heard. A bad case of 'Well, shut ma mouf?'

And then there was . . . but let us turn to other people's disasters – they have them, too. Unforgettable was the night the prima donna in the third act of *Tosca* jumped to her death from the turrets on to the hidden Sorbo mattress, only to bounce back, trampoline-wise, in sight of all the Royal Opera House at Covent Garden.

The night the *Nibelungen* came on – same house, different disaster – shouldering their blocks of gold; all but one. He had shouldered his gold brick back to front and appeared to be processing with a cardboard-coloured square marked ⑤ in black, which referred to his place in the entrée rather than anything dreamed up by Wagner.

The night at Stratford-on-Avon when the very distinguished and fine actor played *Otello* with only half a moustache.

The night (Stratford again) when the lady in the Scottish drama crashed in her sleep-walking scene, sideways from the top of her steep and narrow stairs to the stage below – decidedly an unrehearsed effect.

The night a touring ballet company, too modest to tote around their own orchestra, had a much-tried Swan Princess give the first act of *Swan Lake* to a recording of the second act.

So many disasters jostle my crowded memory but all of them yield to the night I arrived at the Greenwich Theatre where we were giving the Brahms-Sherrin-Grainer musical *Sing a Rude Song* (extra material by Alan Bennett) to find Barbara Windsor (our Marie Lloyd) had sung too many rude songs and had lost her voice. In her stead was Ned Sherrin cueing in Robin Phillips, the director, in sweater and jeans, reading the part.

I needed a double brandy to see me through that disaster.

Martin Lawrence

BASS

I shall always remember a performance of *Don Pasquale* at the Cambridge Theatre in London in the 1940s when I was singing the title role. My Norina fainted as the curtain came down on Act II. Since I was the biggest man on the stage, I picked her up and carried her through to the Green Room. (We still had them in those days. Now, you're more likely to find the space given over to electricians, hat-makers and wig-restorers!)

After some delay Norina was sufficiently recovered for the opera to go on and the curtain duly rose, after a longish interval, on Act III and my duet with Norina in which there is great hurling of abuse.

Doing this convincingly and being in a state of anxiety in case she collapsed again was no easy matter, but happily we got through to the end with nothing else going wrong.

It was only later that the truth came out. . . .

Norina apparently had a lover in the company. Her husband had got to hear of the affair and had been sighted roaming around backstage with, it was alleged, a loaded revolver . . . no one was shot but I can't help but feel anything but gratitude to the people who kept the news from the rest of the cast before the curtain went up.

Tragicomedy

An Italian diva, a bit past her prime perhaps, was having trouble controlling a rowdy Neopolitan audience. The growing noise of catcalls developed into pandemonium while she trudged on gamely, her delivery almost inaudible. Eventually, however, came salvation.

Someone in the stalls stood up and bawled at the gods with a tremendous voice the local equivalent of, 'Why don't you all shut up and give the poor old cow a chance?'

His plea restored some order, which the singer came to the footlights to acknowledge:

'Thank you, sir. It's nice to know there's at least one gentleman in the house.'

Lord Goodman

LAWYER

Rossini was asked to listen to two pieces by a young composer who told him he had to play at a concert in the very near future, and would be most obliged if Rossini would tell him which he liked best. Being a kindly man, Rossini listened to the first piece and then said: 'Don't bother to play the second. I prefer it.'

At a musical soirée in Paris, a soprano sang Rossini's 'Una Voce' in the maestro's presence. She had a magnificent voice and even more facility of execution but unfortunately over-iced the cake with an eccentric display of grace-notes, trills, cadenzas and all the other weapons in the armoury of all virtuoso singers of her time. When she ran out of invention and eventually stopped, Rossini rose to congratulate her on her vocal powers. Then he asked, rather plaintively:
    'But *what* were you singing?'

From the *House of Lords Official Report*.

Metal fatigue

Two seasons ago Raymond Herincx deputized at short notice for Gwynne Howell one evening as Wotan in the English National Opera's acclaimed *Siegfried* in the *Ring* cycle. He coped magnificently with the part but not entirely with Ralph Koltai's metallic set.

As the climax approached in which he was to bar Siegfried's ascent towards Brünnhilde, a misplaced foot sent the lower part of the 'rock' on which he was standing crashing over like a see-saw beneath him.

There was a sharp intake of breath from every part of the house but in spite of a twisted ankle, Herincx kept his balance and continued to sing. His only sign of discomfort was when he presented his spear to be shattered by Alberto Remedios' sword. The release catch disengaged too soon and it exploded early.

His twisted ankle prevented him taking his curtain calls.

[BD: In case you're wondering what this is doing in a book intended to entertain, the punch-line came in the next day's newspapers which reported the incident. Much was made of Herincx's perfect English, references were made to his stepping into a foreign-language role at short notice, one paper went so far as to say he had sung with the English National Opera on previous occasions. Raymond Herincx is English.]

Aubrey Essex

JOURNALIST

Internal memo to the Editor
You will doubtless think me craven. Frankly I no longer care. I am
concerned only with the desire to return to the serenity of the
sports pages, to preserve what is left of my sanity after this trauma-
tic term as your music critic.

Had you not noticed that I now twitch in the office, sometimes
with unfortunate results? The facial spasms have become increasingly misinterpreted, not only by office girls but also by people of
both sexes in the concert hall and opera house, as winks and leers
and unspoken invitations to do something wicked. But worse than
this, my hearing – my already *power-assisted* hearing – is deteriorat-
ing rapidly. The volume control on my deaf-aid is now at maximum but the sound of music is fading. Perhaps that is a blessing in
itself. But the fact is that this dreadful deafness is the direct result of
years of bombardment by opera.

Too many Toscas have made me vertiginous. Too many Mimis
have frozen my otitis media. Too many Aidas have entombed my
tympanum. I have become dyspeptic through having too many
Madam Butterflies in my stomach. It has become so intolerable
that, in one of my recent moments of shrieking madness, I
destroyed my wife's priceless collection of 78s, every one an irre-
placeable gem. Caruso singing as though with his head in the gas
oven; Gigli's chocolate Neopolitans; Tauber's tortured English – all
gone, reduced to a black shellac jigsaw puzzle on our living-room
carpet.

I was never really cut out to be a critic of opera. That I became one
at all was some sort of cosmic joke. If you cannot recall the circumstances of my appointment, I shall remind you. It was the première

production of that brilliant West Midlands company, which had resurrected the little-performed *Sicilian Vespers* presumably to prove why it had been performed so little. The work was as familiar to me then as *Rigoletto* would be to a punk rocker now. I, in those humble days of junior sports-hack, had always secretly yearned more for the press box at White Hart Lane than the stalls at the London Coliseum. But at that terrible turning-point of my career, I found myself among the many complimentary ticket-holders, and, since the First Division side was playing away that evening, I thought the opera would provide an interesting if bizarre, evening.

I remember sitting in row G, surrounded by my editorial colleagues, waiting for kick-off. In the event, the match was started by a tail-suited referee who hammered twice with his stick on the back of a piano and drew a hesitant response from a forward-line of fiddlers who seem to have started not quite together. The curtains parted and I was watching my first professional opera.

What strange creatures these were, I thought, whose faces hung heavy with make-up, whose expressions of uniform melancholy had been trowelled on, and whose ponderous movements suggested that the stage had mysteriously acquired the gravitational pull of a quasar. Eyes flashed signals from mounds of mascara. Arms smote brows and bosoms, the latter particularly ample.

But even I, for all my ignorance of this art form, was stunned by the range, the power, the clarity, the definition of the voices. For a moment, I believed I understood Italian and it was only later on in the evening I found that the work was being given in English.

Two rows ahead of me, in row E, I saw the glistening dome of the venerated critic of your newspaper, that musical Methuselah so soon to join the masters, nodding approval and wagging a finger in perfect rapport with the conductor.

Do you remember the horror that followed? Some moments into the second half, it was, as night was falling in Sicily and a chilling bell tolled the fears of hell. Suddenly your critic groaned, loud enough to bring the front row of dress circle heads craning over the parapet, rose in his seat, flung his arms towards the gallery, and then with all the authority and finality of his seventy-six years, collapsed over the lady in row D, impaling himself on her tiara.

Personally, though no expert, I hadn't thought the performance was all *that* bad.

On-stage a formidable large contralto cast a single withering glance in the direction of your critic's demonstration, and then continued doggedly as two St John Ambulance men raced along the aisle, laying about them with a stretcher.

With the moaning departure of your much-loved critic, unease rustled among the remaining complimentary ticket-holders on your staff.

The question arose, inevitably, in all minds: who, within the hour or so remaining before our presses rolled would write the necessary half a column of constructive criticism based on knowledge and experience of opera?

I saw you looking about from your seat in row F. I bowed my head, ostensibly to investigate a point in the programme. I looked up – to find my gaze locked into yours. You had made up your mind.

I knew the worst.

Me.

It was I who should write the notice.

Next morning's headlines: 'NEW COMPANY SCORES WITH RARE OPERA' alongside 'DEATH OF REVERED CRITIC' did nothing to dispel my fears that coincidence might be about to play an important role in my career. In the event, I was right.

It was only yesterday that a new touring group announced they were bringing us the little-performed *Sicilian Vespers*. That, I am afraid, has confirmed my decision to quit.

In any case, I cannot face the prospect of *Opera 81*, if only because it will be followed inevitably by *Opera 82, 83* and so on. *Opera for All* was without equal, a laudable ideal, so long as it remained *Opera for All the Others*.

Please, may I now go back to the obscurity of the back page?

Poppaea in Glasgow

That the production did not run as smoothly as it might may well have been due to the May Day strike resulting in absent stage staff.

In the first of the scenes in Poppaea's bedroom, two stage-hands did not get out of the way quickly enough as the curtain went up and were left marooned, though by no means invisible, behind the bed.

Their presence and the fact that the bed was not properly anchored and kept moving round the stage added considerably to the miseries that Nero and Poppaea had to face.

At the end of the act the bed refused to leave the stage at all with the two ostensibly nude bodies on it and a scene the producer intended should be sensuous became a comic interlude.

[BD: Somebody sitting in the gods told me they could see even more. What *can* they have meant?]

The missing maestro

It was past time for the curtain to rise at Covent Garden. A strained House Manager appeared on stage to tell the waiting audience that the performance of *Die Fledermaus* unfortunately could not begin. There was, he explained, no conductor.

At that very moment, the missing maestro, Zubin Mehta, was being driven at speed through the London traffic, bound for the Opera House. Ten minutes before he had been sleeping peacefully in his hotel room, dreaming perhaps of Puccini and *La Fanciulla del West* which he had been rehearsing that morning. He would probably have slept much longer had it not been for an anxious alarm call from the Garden, asking if he intended to conduct that evening's performance.

Meanwhile, back at the Opera House, it so happened that one of the members of the audience anxiously rustling his programme was Placido Domingo who is something of an authority on *Die Fledermaus*. Placido, who has often declared a longing to become a conductor, had indeed saved the day at Munich when he conducted the opera on New Year's Eve in place of Carlos Kleiber who was unable to go on at the last moment. All eyes turned to him as he rose to his feet and made a dramatic exit from the auditorium. Excitedly, the audience wondered if he would re-emerge clutching a baton. Sadly for Domingo, Mehta at that moment rushed into the orchestra pit and the performance eventually began – fifteen minutes late.

Out of consideration for the folk who had trains to catch Mehta managed to make up seven minutes by accelerating Acts I and II, and by Act III his late arrival had been written into the libretto. The final comment came from Michael Langdon, who, as Prison

Governor, took out his watch to announce the time. Turning to the pit, Langdon called out in English:

'Seven-thirty. And you,' he cried, pointing at Mehta, 'were not here till a quarter to eight!'

From Londoner's Diary, *Evening Standard*, 11 January 1978.

Robinson Caruso

Caruso pulled up in a small town in America for petrol. 'Say,' said the attendant in amazement, 'aren't you Caruso?'

The great tenor had to admit that he was.

'Jeez!' said the man. 'Wait till I tell the wife. I've just served the great Robinson Caruso himself.'

One day he went into a barber shop in New York where the proprietor fawned over him dreadfully: 'And how is the world's greatest tenor this morning?'

'You mean John McCormack died?' replied Caruso.

On stage Caruso could not resist the opportunity for comedy whenever it arose, no matter what the part or opera. Once at the Met his pistol in *La Forza del Destino*, failed to go off when he threw it at the Marchese's feet, thereby failing to dispose of the Marchese.

Grinning broadly, Caruso turned to the audience and said, in English: 'Bang! Bang!'

Sir Rudolph Bing

DIRECTOR, METROPOLITAN OPERA HOUSE

There is an Austrian saying that things work themselves out but I am Austrian and it isn't so. The massive overtime costs and the cost of overruns on the new productions (which were not just tens, but *hundreds* of thousands of dollars over budget) raised serious problems. . . .

We continued to explore the possibilities for added income. New productions became Guild benefits at higher prices, and there were frequent galas to benefit the house. In 1964 we made a deal with National General, a new Hollywood film-producing company, to make a movie of our production of *Turandot* with Nilsson, Price and Corelli, each of whom was ultimately paid $5,000 for his or her courtesy in granting an option for a film National General finally decided not to make.

Many of these ideas were just foolish. George Moore came back from his house in Spain in 1968 with a neighbour who is a film director, both of them very excited about making a movie of *La Bohème* set in the Paris student revolt. I said:

'Where are there two bars of revolutionary music in *La Bohème*? What music is there to throw rocks by? You can't add music to a Puccini opera, not with the Metropolitan name on it while I am general manager of the Metropolitan.'

With the accession of George Moore and the return of the bankers to a dominant position on the Metropolitan board, we were once again concentrating on mass-communication gimmickry that should somehow solve all our problems. Endless hours of negotiating went on with all the unions so that we could offer Metropolitan productions for television again – at a hoped-for profit to the company, if all went well, of $25,000 for each of the two performances.

There was much talk and much negotiating about cable television, TV cassettes and other miraculous devices. I hope I can be pardoned for not believing in it.

Together with the prayerful invocation of such outside revenues there came a renewal of ignorant attacks on me and my associates for our alleged wastefulness. I was always being asked why we trimmed our costumes with real fur, when of course we *didn't* trim our costumes with real fur, or why the chorus ladies wore real diamonds, when of course there wasn't a costume in the house where the jewellery was anything but glass or plastic.

The greatest singers of the world don't fit easily into blue jeans. It takes a great effort to clothe Monserrat Caballé well, and that effort must always be expensive. Also, a high order of sturdiness is necessary for any costume that is going to have to be packed up in trunks right after each use on the Metropolitan spring tour. In truth, the best quality is the cheapest way for the Metropolitan to produce opera over the long run: the price of Eugene Berman's *Rigoletto* costumes scandalized my board in 1951, but we were still

using these costumes, and they still looked good, after well over a hundred wearings in 1972. Ultimately, as I kept telling the board, if the Metropolitan Opera wishes to put on City Opera productions, it will have to charge City Opera rather than Metropolitan Opera prices.

Moore could not believe there is a basic unbridgeable difference between a theatre and a bank or a rug factory, because the human element is a hundred thousand per cent more at an opera house. He sent around poor fellows who had never been on a stage before to analyse every motion anybody made on the stage. They were there for weeks, at a cost of thousands of dollars, following the men around – and finally they had little to recommend.

From *5000 Nights at the Opera* by Sir Rudolph Bing (Hamish Hamilton 1972).

Lucienne Hill

PLAYWRIGHT AND TRANSLATOR OF MANY OF JEAN ANOUILH'S PLAYS

I'll never get over my rapture, really, at just *sitting* in an opera house and I don't believe I would notice if anything were to go wrong.

I used to go a lot with Barry Jackson [Sir Barry Jackson, founder of the Birmingham Repertory Theatre] and I remember his giggling most of the way through *Boris Godonov* (with Boris *Christoff* of course) because Christoff kept waving this immense handkerchief about and Barry snorted: 'Fellow's forgotten his napkin ring' – which was really his way of hiding his immense love of music and drama.

'Goodness,' I thought, 'will I ever get to be as sophisticated as that?'

Well. No. I never did.

John Mortimer

BARRISTER, PLAYWRIGHT AND AUTHOR

I was on my way to the first night of *Luisa Miller* at Covent Garden when I stopped for petrol at a garage in Park Lane. Months before, the North Country pump attendant there told me he had seen me in the seats behind him at *Aida*. When I asked him if he didn't find the stalls rather expensive at Covent Garden, he said they cost no more than any other pump man spent on a 'piss-up' on Friday nights. Now he fixed the nozzle into my tank and said, 'Let me tell you about *Rigoletto*.'

'I know,' I said, 'The tenor got booed.'

'Not that! It's that Wixell! When he sang my hands trembled with excitement. Of course, I know all about Wagner. I've got the records. My brother's going to Bayreuth, isn't he? Wagner may have been a great man of the theatre but Verdi's the boy for me!'

By this time, the line of Rolls-Royce chauffeurs waiting for petrol were honking their horns in fury.

Perhaps they were all addicts of *The Ring*.

In the backstage canteen at the Royal Opera, the feeling of a subterranean air-raid shelter is ameliorated by a small bar, ham salad and roly-poly. The ballet dancers sit in silent suffering, the singers talk incessantly.

'Of course,' said one, 'operas have different audiences. With Mozart you get the musicologists so there's a constant rustling of scores.'

'Wagner audiences are the kinkiest,' said another.

'How kinky?' I asked.

'Either outrageous. Or else bank managers in striped suits absolutely bursting to be Siegfried.'

'I'll tell you kinkier audiences than that,' a third singer added.

'Which?' I enquired.

'For any Strauss opera where you get a girl dressed as a boy who pretends to be a girl. That turns the sopranos on too. They get wonderfully excited.'

'Bass singers are family men on the whole,' said Robert Lloyd, a big bearded ex-police lecturer, who was understudying Count Walter in *Luisa Miller*, a job he regards as a necessary chore for a regular salaried singer: something he feels he owes the Opera House in return for letting him off to undertake frequent roles abroad.

'Tenors are far more promiscuous – it must be the strain of all those high notes.'

'When I was in the Deep South,' said Richard Van Allan, 'the whole girls' chorus in *Rosenkavalier* were male amateurs in drag. After the show they used to get dated by huge traffic cops.'

Sergeant Martin, the imposing uniformed figure to be seen outside the Royal Opera House and inside the foyer keeping order, takes a more traditional view of audiences.

'I do like to see evening dress, I must confess. I like to see a nice lounge suit. At bare feet, I draw the line.

'The other night, in this foyer, I saw some on a young lady. I went up to her and I said: "If you cut your toes on a broken glass in the Crush Bar, miss, don't come crying to Sergeant Martin."

'I think she got the message.'

Sitting it out

Renato Gigli was singing the lead in *Otello* at the Lisbon Opera when he slightly mis-timed a piece of business – the producer had asked him to throw himself down heavily into a chair in the middle of an impassioned aria in order to register disgust.

And so he did – on a huge backless stool midstage. But so passionately, so disgustedly, he fell over the back of it, leaving his boots pointing straight up into the flies.

But only for a moment. Still singing, he rolled over sideways, staggered to his feet and continued as if he always sang the aria like that. He acknowledged the applause with smiling good grace.

[BD: A bit like the story of Bernard Shaw who, having fallen all the way down the underground escalator at Leicester Square, stood up at the bottom and tried to look as if he always went down that way.]

Pauline Grant

DANCE AND MOVEMENT CONSULTANT, ENGLISH NATIONAL OPERA

My work for the English National Opera often necessitates frequent hurried backstage visits during performances, either to remind the Movement Group of recent alterations, or to query strange choreographic 'improvements' which have a habit of creeping in after first night.

My eyes re-orientate particularly sluggishly to darkness and I had been complaining bitterly to Ruth Anders, the General Stage Manager, of the difficulty I was having in groping blindly through the gloom of the cable-littered wings. Usually, Ruth's soothing voice and a carefully-lowered torch came to my assistance, but one night, during *Trovatore*, when the sins of the ballet seemed to me to be more heinous than usual, I rushed precipitately through the pass door and within seconds was enveloped in what seemed like acres of stifling black velvet. The more I struggled, the more I became enmeshed. Clawing and fighting, I gasped:

'Ruth! Quick! Get me out of here! I'm caught in the black tabs!'

'Oh, no you're not, you know!' a well-known voice, succinct and unruffled answered directly above my head – 'it's *me!*'

I surfaced out on to an accommodating bosom which proceeded, dead on cue, into a magnificent Act IV entrance: Rita Hunter.

Kenneth Robinson

BROADCASTER AND CRITIC

When I hear all those radio request tunes I can't help feeling that some people must surely have their favourite hates as well – their desert island discards.

At the top of my own list is 'Love and Music' from *Tosca*. I quite liked this number until I heard it sung by an extravagant soprano with a temperament to match. I was touring with her at the time and, night after night, as we entertained the troops, she would take exception to something said backstage. Then, white with passion, she would stagger out to her audience with a wisp of a handkerchief clutched in one hand and the top of the piano in the other.

I can never hear this lovely music without remembering what I felt like while accompanying it, with one foot tucked round the corner of the piano in case the quivering coloratura really did collapse, as she had threatened. Every time I hear the first few bars, even now, I move into a sprinting position, ready to catch the singer if necessary.

This was my only encounter with opera, apart from the time I did an audition for Leonard Urry's Discoveries at the Royal Opera House, Covent Garden. It was a dance hall in those war-time days and I still cannot believe that I accompanied Al Bowlly in that magnificent setting for a few bars of something that went – in that evening's version – 'over the rainbow, way up high, thank you sonny, we'll let you know'.

But I digress. Another of my desert island discards is Strauss's 'Voices of Spring'. It is a jolly enough piece but not something I care to listen to these days. It brings back memories of a war-time concert I took part in at an RAF base. As we, Kenneth Robinson's Golden Strings, assembled for the opening bars of Strauss a corporal appeared to stick the white tops back on the keys. The keyboard looked like a huge smile full of decayed teeth.

Would the tops stay in place? Of course, said the corporal, he had used the very best glue. We swung into action. Too late I felt the tops of the keys beginning to move. It was impossible to turn back. The Golden Strings played on bravely. At first both Joyce, from Forest Gate, and Brenda (ah, Brenda!), from Harpenden, ignored me as my notes slithered over one another in a congealing mess. At least it was different. Today you could get away with it by blowing a whistle at the same time and saying it was experimental.

Fortunately I had the presence of mind to consult the Golden Strings, and we switched quickly to Handel's 'Largo'. This lovely melody has the advantage of sounding like a prolonged vamp-till-ready. So I thought there was a chance to play with the left hand only while the right hand picked off the loose top notes and threw them away. At first the loose bits of white stuck to my fingers and then – as I tried to brush them off – to my waistcoat. I even managed to hit one that was creeping over the edge of the piano. It flew backwards into the front row and the VIPs then bounced harmlessly into the other ranks. It was only when the keyboard was cleared of débris that I realized my mistake. Instead of loose notes I now had a lot of very sticky key-bases that came up with the fingers after every chord. The Handel turned out twice as long as usual, with a plopping obbligato. I can still hear those 'gedoinks' when the wretched thing is played.

There are several other tunes I don't want to hear again, all because of the memory of grotesque pianos. Most of the instruments I met on tour had something wrong with the right pedal. Either they didn't work at all, thus destroying the opening bars of Tchaikovsky's *No. 1* (and I only played the opening bars), or they worked all the time, spoiling the crisp and subtle nuances of 'The Teddy Bears' Picnic'. So those, as you might guess, are two more tunes for my desert island discards.

I did in fact devise a way of mending piano pedals with sock suspenders. You may remember those sensuous-looking accessories filled with elastic. They used to trap the hair behind the knees and make you scream as you came downstairs in the morning. One day I was fitting a sock suspender in a piano when something snapped and the whole upper register went silent. This happened just before 'The Blue Danube' which meant that the audience got 'O Danube so blue, thud-thud, so blue'. That became another of my discards. I spent the entire concert trying to think of a composition to be played in the lower register that was not 'The Dead March'. This, I felt, would be inappropriate as we were performing in a hospital ward.

The saddest moment of my musical career came when the piano was perfect but there was something missing. I didn't know at the time there was anything wrong, but the television producer told me as she finished giving me my audition. The new and exciting medium of television, she said, required more than mere talent. Good though my rendering had been, my act was not mobile enough. With dreadful sarcasm I asked if she would have liked a girl draped on the piano lid. That, she said, was exactly the sort of thing television would be looking for.

It was too much for me. After all those years of concealing suspenders *inside* the piano I could never have brought myself to decorate the outside with them as well. It was all over. Never again would I want to play 'Meet me in the Valley of Never-Say-When'.

You will not know the tune, because it became one of my discards and was never heard again. It was in fact my very own composition and it had been personally rejected by Glenn Miller, Ivy Benson, Turner Layton and Cavan O'Connor. It was Paul McCartney who summed up for everybody. 'They don't write tunes like that today,' I said when I unearthed it for him twenty-five years later. 'What's more', he said, 'they never did.'

Lord Barnetson

CHAIRMAN, UNITED NEWSPAPERS LIMITED

I had been given tickets for a performance but unfortunately could not use them so I passed them on to one of my Work Study Consultants. The next morning, I asked him how he had enjoyed the evening. Instead of a few plausible observations, he handed me a memorandum which read:

(a) For considerable periods, the four oboe players had nothing to do. The number should be reduced and their work spread over the whole orchestra, thus eliminating peaks of activity.

(b) All the twelve violins were playing identical notes. This seems unnecessary duplication and the staff of this section should be cut drastically. If a large volume of sound is really required, this could be obtained through an electronic amplifier.

(c) Much effort was absorbed in the playing of demisemiquavers. This seems an excessive requirement and it is recommended that all notes should be rounded up to the nearest semiquaver. If this were done it should be possible to use trainees and lower grade operators.

(d) No useful purpose is served by repeating with horns the passage that has already been handled by the strings. If all such redundant passages were eliminated, the piece could be cut from two hours to twenty minutes.

Tony Cross

STAGE-HAND

I was working at the Bristol Hippodrome when the Carl Rosa took in a production of *Madam Butterfly*. One of my jobs was to gently waft almond petals about Butterfly as she sang one of her arias. The petals were made from torn up paper and fell through a hole in a cardboard box tied with string to the end of a long bamboo pole which was waved out of sight above the prima donna from behind a flat.

One night the string broke. The cardboard box fell from its pole and hit Butterfly on the head. She finished her aria shuffling through paper petals, cardboard and string. I would rather not say what happened to me.

My father was a St John Ambulance officer and thoroughly enjoyed being on duty at Covent Garden. He was never to forget Eva Turner's farewell performance as Turandot. She was unwell at the time and was grateful that the St John's man was ready to receive her at each of her exits, collapsing into his arms at the end of her every scene.

For my father this was his most exhausting opera ever. He was only five feet two inches tall and subsequently came to regard the complete *Ring* cycle as light opera.

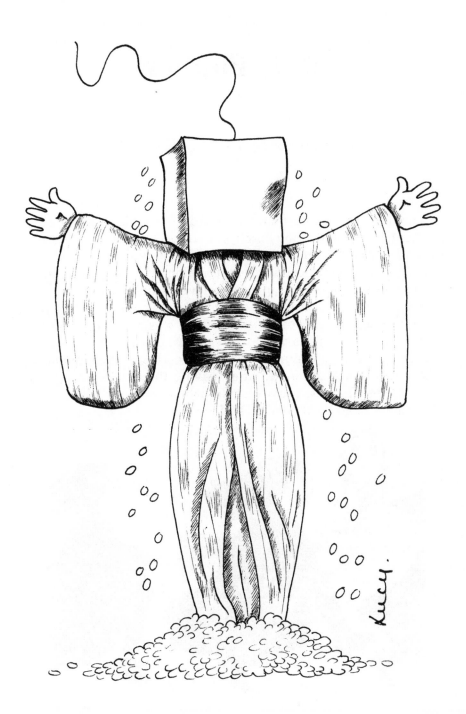

R. L. Poulter

ORGANIST AND CHOIR-MASTER

I remember going to a matinée of *Tosca* at Sadler's Wells on 7 September 1940 and being much amused by Tosca's annoyance at the end of Act II when the candles resolutely refused to be blown out. They may have been some sort of omen but the performance and its date have remained in my memory for quite another reason.

It was announced from the stage that an air-raid warning had been sounded – and because of this there was no 'bang' from the soldiers' rifles when Cavaradossi was shot. He just fell down.

Warnings were a common occurrence earlier in the summer of 1940 but this was different. After leaving the theatre and going down to the Thames, I saw that the whole riverside was ablaze. The railways had been bombed and we managed to get a bus from

Victoria coach station only much later in the evening by which time the sky all over London was red with flame.

[BD: The blitz had begun. The theatre closed. For a year it became home for about two hundred people whose own homes had been destroyed. It reopened on Thursday 7 July 1945 with *Peter Grimes*.]

Thirty-five years later, at another performance of *Tosca*, there was a bomb hoax which caused the Coliseum to be evacuated. Onlookers relished the expression on the faces of the people in St Martin's Lane as three nuns dashed out of the stage door straight into the Lemon Tree pub.

Finale

[BD: The last word must come from Lilian Bayliss, founder of Sadler's Wells Company from which sprang the English National Opera and the Royal Ballet.]

At the time when she opened Sadler's Wells in 1931 Lilian Bayliss was given to driving sonething pretty lethal called a Trojan (motor-car) round London which was dangerous not only to herself but to practically everybody else on the road as well.

When the inevitable crash came a rescuer recognized her as she was hauled from the wreckage.

'Why!' he exclaimed. 'It's Miss Bayliss of the Old Vic!'

Whereupon that indomitable lady rallied immediately to point out:

'*And* Sadler's Wells!'

The English National Opera and Sadler's Wells Benevolent Fund

The English National Opera and Sadler's Wells Benevolent Fund, to which the proceeds of *A Night at the Opera* are to go, exists for serving and retired artists and staff. It is a registered charity and operates under a Charity Commission scheme administered by four trustees – two appointed by the board of the English National Opera (Miss Joanna Smith and Miss Sheila Scotter MBE) and two by the governors of the Sadler's Wells Foundation (Mr Leopold de Rothschild and Sir Roger Falk OBE). Miss Joanna Smith is the present chairman. The Fund's office is at the London Coliseum.

The original Sadler's Wells Benevolent Fund was established in 1956 with a modest capital and the primary aim of providing small pensions for the relatively few people who had sustained the company through the years of the Second World War and immediately afterwards. From 1956 to 1972 a number of pensions were started, but because of the very limited funds it was possible to maintain them only through a considerable grant from the Sadler's Wells Trust. It was then decided to develop separate resources with the aim of making it independent of the grant from the Trust. This was achieved from 1974 onwards and, at the same time, the present Fund title was adopted. Though the English National Opera Trust no longer makes a grant, it still bears the cost of administration.

The two purposes of the fund remain unchanged – to provide pensions to supplement the state retirement pension for those who cannot be covered through company pension schemes, and grants to alleviate sudden misfortune or hardship. Some of the pensioners are more than eighty years old and in most cases have served the company for thirty years or more. Grants have been made to help in a wide variety of circumstances: to a singer no longer able to work following an operation; to another who had to stop work for six months for special treatment; to a member of staff obliged to be away from the Coliseum for some months in order to look after his sick wife – and to many more faced with unexpected hardship. Grants are also given to those who have to move home, or are bedridden (one has multiple sclerosis and the fund has given a television set and continuing help with extra needs for her comfort). Help has been forthcoming for extra heating, household repairs and equipment.

The Fund's outgoings increase every year through inflation and new pensions, and in 1980–1, the total expenditure is expected to be around £27,000. About one-third of this is covered by investment income but the aim is to increase this during the coming years. Meanwhile, the remaining two-thirds must be found from fund-raising – gala performances, film premières, covenants and donations.

The need for the Fund is continuing and real. Its work helps to fill a very important gap. If you would like to contribute, please write to:

Colonel J. L. A. Guy,
Secretary,
English National Opera & Sadler's Wells Benevolent Fund,
London Coliseum,
St Martin's Lane,
London WC2N 4ES

Acknowledgements

Putting together a book of this sort involves using a certain amount of copyright material. Wherever possible I have contacted the owners of the copyright; if I have unwittingly committed an infringement I hereby apologize and will gladly rectify the omission in any future reprint, provided notification is received.

For permission to quote copyright passages I should like to express my gratitude to the *Daily Telegraph*, *Evening Standard*, the *Guardian*, *New Statesman*, the *Observer Colour Magazine*, the *Savoyard*; Doubleday and Company, Leslie Frewin Books Limited, Hamish Hamilton Limited, Woolfe Publishing Limited; Joyce Grenfell, the Society of Authors on behalf of the Bernard Shaw Estate, Patrick Fyffe and George Logan.

Joyce Grenfell's 'Opera Interval' and the interview with Hinge and Bracket are fully protected by copyright and may not be performed.

My special thanks to Janet.

I am very grateful to all those who helped, encouraged and advised me, especially the following: M. R. Abbs, Dr H. D. Apergis, Sir Robert Armstrong CB CVO, Mollie Ashworth, David Attenborough, Marjorie K. Bagnall, Dame Janet Baker DBE, Mrs A. G. Bates, Eva Balthazar, Sir Ian Bancroft GCB, Shirley Lady Beecham, Jessica Bonnin, A. M. J. Bove, Ivor Brecker, S. J. Breeze, J. Bretherton, Mary Brough, Gordon Burrett CB, R. Burrows, Mrs C. Cardozo, H. A. Chambers, Brian B. Clifford, Brigadier John Commings CBE, Mrs C. S. Compton. Roger Cursley, Ann Daly, Janet Dunbar, Constance Edwards, N. Eisner, Jon Evans, Glenn Fabry, J. B. Fielding, Marion Fleischer, J. Forsdick, Mrs D. C. Freeman, G. Walter George, Olive Gilbert, Dr J. L. Gleave, Sir Reginald Goodall, Jamie Gray, Sir Charles Groves, Mrs L. Gudgeon,

Colonel J. L. A. Guy, N. C. Harridge, Pam Hawken, Ralph Henley, Peter Hillier, Lily Hoffman, Richard Hopkins, the Rt Hon. Denis Howell MP, Muriel Huck, Rex Hudson, Elizabeth Hughes, Simon Jenkins, Antoinette Johnson, George Johnson, Fred Jones, Nicholas Jones, Nan Kerin-Walker, Lieutenant-Colonel Boris Klukvin, Miss E. M. Knight, Mary Konstan, B. A. Kopkin, Faith Krawczk, Rafael Kubelik, Michael Langdon, Margaret Lazarides, Laurie Lee, Peter Longhurst, Mrs L. Maynard, Doris McDonald, June McKay, P. N. Meats, Harry Miller, Polly Mills, Evan Morris, Patrick Moore, Margaret O'Brien, Eileen Palmer, Wilfred Payne, Susan Pegg, H. G. Phillips, Lois Potter, Peter Pratt, K. A. Prett, R. C. Preston, Gilbert Price, Miss I. Prebble, Richard Prior, Kenneth Radley, John Ralls, Sheila Redgrave, Connie Riordan, D. J. Roberts, John T. Roberts, Miss L. H. Roberts, David Robinson, the Rev. Gordon Robinson, Donald Ross, Chris Rudden, Dean Sadlers, Helen Salomon, H. Sanders, Hugh Sawbridge, Surgeon Commander F. G. V. Scovell, Miss C. Shepherd, Miss P. Shepherd, Barbara Smith, Colin Smith, Joan Smith, Violet Campbell Southam, A. N. Sparke, C. E. Stewart, James Stewart, Jennifer Stock, George Taylor, Dorothy Turner, Mrs E. J. Tyler, W. H. Wagstaff, Francis Weiss, George Wheatley, Donald Wintersgill, Geoffrey Wilson, Susan Wilson, Norman Wylie, Alec Yearling.